ANTHONY FORBES

# Commercial Real Estate for Beginners

*How Anyone Can Achieve Stress-Free, Profitable Investments*

First edition

This book was professionally typeset on Reedsy.
Find out more at reedsy.com

# Contents

# 1

# Introduction

## Welcome to Commercial Real Estate Investing for Beginners!

### Introduction

Thank you for choosing our self-guided text-based course on commercial real estate investing for beginners. We are excited to have you on board as you embark on this journey to explore the world of commercial real estate and learn how to make informed investment decisions.

Commercial real estate investing offers a unique opportunity to diversify your investment portfolio and potentially generate significant returns. Whether you are a novice investor looking to get started or someone with prior experience in real estate, this course is designed to provide you with a comprehensive foundation in commercial real estate investing.

Over the course of this program, you will gain a deep understanding of the fundamental concepts, strategies, and key factors that drive success in commercial real estate investing. From analyzing market trends and evaluating different property types to assessing financial risks and maximizing returns, we will cover it all.

Through a combination of informative lessons, practical examples, and interactive exercises, you will develop the knowledge and skills necessary to make sound investment decisions in the commercial real estate sector. Our aim is to empower you with the tools and insights needed to navigate this complex industry confidently.

We understand that everyone learns at their own pace, which is why this self-guided course allows you to learn on your schedule and at your convenience. You can access the course materials anytime, anywhere, making it ideal for busy individuals who want to enhance their financial literacy and explore new investment avenues.

So, whether you aspire to invest in office buildings, retail centers, industrial properties, or any other type of commercial real estate, this course will equip you with the essential knowledge to kickstart your journey. Get ready to dive into the exciting world of commercial real estate investing!

Let's begin!

1. Finding Profitable Real Estate Deals: Learn how to identify and analyze potential investment properties to maximize your returns.
2. Understanding Real Estate Market Trends: Gain insights into market dynamics and learn how to spot opportunities and potential risks.
3. Learning the Basics of Real Estate Investing: Get a com-

prehensive overview of the fundamental concepts and strategies used in real estate investing.

4. Identifying Potential Risks in Real Estate Investing: Understand the various risks associated with real estate investments and learn how to mitigate them.

5. Building a Strong Real Estate Investment Portfolio: Discover strategies for diversifying your portfolio and selecting properties that align with your investment goals.

6. Securing Financing for Real Estate Investments: Learn about different financing options available to real estate investors and how to navigate the lending process.

7. Developing a Real Estate Investment Strategy: Create a personalized investment plan based on your financial goals, risk tolerance, and market conditions.

8. Navigating Legal and Regulatory Requirements: Understand the legal and regulatory framework governing real estate investments and ensure compliance.

9. Maximizing Cash Flow from Real Estate Investments: Learn strategies to increase rental income, reduce expenses, and optimize your cash flow.

10. Networking with Experienced Real Estate Investors: Discover the importance of building a network and learn how to connect with experienced investors for guidance and collaboration.

## Conclusion

Congratulations on taking the first step towards your journey in commercial real estate investing!

By purchasing this self-guided text-based course, you have demonstrated your determination and commitment to learning the ins and outs of commercial real estate. Now, it's time to put that motivation into action and embark on your exciting investment journey.

Throughout this course, you will gain a comprehensive understanding of the fundamentals of commercial real estate investing. From analyzing potential properties to negotiating deals, you will learn the essential skills needed to make informed investment decisions.

Remember, knowledge is power, but action is what drives results. It's not enough to simply read and absorb the course material; you must apply what you learn. Take advantage of the practical exercises and real-world examples provided to hone your skills and build your confidence as a beginner commercial real estate investor.

Don't be afraid to step outside of your comfort zone and take calculated risks. Investing in commercial real estate can be a lucrative venture if approached with the right mindset and strategy. Trust in your abilities, and remember that every successful investor started somewhere just like you.

As you progress through this course, stay curious and eager to learn. Engage with your fellow course participants through discussion forums and seek guidance from professionals in the field. Surround yourself with a network of like-minded individuals who can support and inspire you on your investment journey.

Now, it's time to dive in and get started. Take full advantage of the valuable resources and knowledge provided in this course. Challenge yourself, ask questions, and never stop learning. The possibilities in commercial real estate investing are endless, and with dedication and perseverance, you can achieve your financial goals.

Remember, success may not come overnight, but with each step you take, you are one step closer to realizing your dreams. So, let's begin this exciting adventure in commercial real estate investing together.

Best of luck on your journey!

# 2

# Find Profitable Real Estate Deals

Welcome to our self-guided lesson on commercial real estate investing for beginners!

If you are someone who is interested in investing in real estate, specifically in the commercial sector, you have come to the right place. This lesson is designed to provide you with the knowledge and tools you need to find profitable real estate deals in the commercial market.

Investing in commercial real estate can be a lucrative venture, but it requires careful research, analysis, and decision-making. Whether you are a seasoned investor looking to expand your portfolio or a beginner taking your first steps into the world of real estate investing, this lesson will guide you through the process.

Our comprehensive lesson will cover various aspects of commercial real estate investing, including understanding market trends, identifying potential investment opportunities, conducting due diligence, evaluating risk and return, and negotiating deals. We will also provide you with practical tips and strategies to help you navigate the complex world of commercial real estate.

By the end of this lesson, you will have a solid understanding of how to find profitable real estate deals in the commercial sector. You will be equipped with the knowledge and skills to make informed investment decisions and maximize your returns.

So, let's get started on this exciting journey to find profitable real estate deals in the commercial market!

Understanding the Basics of Commercial Real Estate Investing

Before diving into the world of commercial real estate investing, it is crucial to have a solid understanding of the basics. This knowledge will help you make informed decisions and increase your chances of finding profitable real estate deals. In this section, we will cover the key concepts and factors that you need to know as a beginner investor.

**1. Types of Commercial Real Estate:**

Commercial real estate encompasses a wide range of properties, including office buildings, retail spaces, industrial warehouses, and multi-family apartment complexes. Each type has its own unique characteristics and potential for returns. Take the time to research and understand the different types to determine which aligns with your investment goals.

**2. Market Analysis:**

Conducting a thorough market analysis is essential when seeking profitable real estate deals. This involves studying local market trends, vacancy rates, rental rates, and economic indicators. By understanding the current state of the market, you can identify areas with high growth potential and where demand for commercial properties is strong.

**3. Financial Analysis:**

Financial analysis plays a critical role in evaluating the profitability of a commercial real estate investment. Key financial metrics to consider include cash flow, net operating income (NOI), cap rate, and return on investment (ROI). Learning how to analyze these numbers will help you assess the potential income and value appreciation of a property.

### 4. Due Diligence:

Before finalizing any real estate deal, it is essential to conduct thorough due diligence. This involves researching the property's history, inspecting the physical condition, reviewing lease agreements, and analyzing the financial records. Due diligence helps uncover any potential issues, such as hidden costs or legal complications, ensuring you make an informed investment decision.

### 5. Risk Assessment:

Every investment carries some level of risk, and commercial real estate is no exception. As a beginner investor, it is crucial to assess and manage these risks effectively. Consider factors such as market volatility, tenant turnover, potential property value fluctuations, and financing risks. Understanding and mitigating these risks will help protect your investment and increase your chances of profitability.

By understanding these basics of commercial real estate investing, you will be better equipped to identify and evaluate profitable real estate deals. Remember to continue learning and staying up-to-date with market trends and industry developments to enhance your investment strategies.

Identifying profitable real estate markets and property types is crucial when it comes to successful commercial real estate investing. By focusing on the right markets and property types, you increase your chances of finding lucrative deals that can generate significant returns on your investment.

Here are some key factors to consider when identifying prof-itable real estate markets:

1. Economic Growth: Look for markets with a strong and growing economy. Areas with increasing job opportunities, population growth, and thriving industries tend to have higher demand for commercial real estate, resulting in potential profitability.
2. Population and Demographics: Consider the population size and demographics of a market. Higher population numbers can indicate a larger customer base for busi-nesses, while demographics such as age, income levels, and lifestyle preferences can help you identify the types of properties that would be in demand.
3. Infrastructure and Development: Assess the quality of infrastructure in a market, including transportation net-works, utilities, and public amenities. Areas with well-developed infrastructure tend to attract businesses and tenants, making them more likely to generate profitable real estate deals.
4. Market Trends and Forecasts: Stay informed about market trends and forecasts. Research reports and data from reputable sources can provide insights into which markets are expected to experience growth and increased demand in the future.

Once you've identified a profitable market, it's important to consider the property types that can offer the best returns. Here are some property types to explore:

1. Office Buildings: Commercial office spaces can be highly profitable in markets with a strong business presence. Look for areas with growing industries and demand for office spaces.

2. Retail Spaces: Retail properties in prime locations with high foot traffic are often sought-after. Consider markets with a thriving retail sector and popular shopping destinations.

3. Industrial Properties: Industrial properties, such as warehouses and manufacturing facilities, can be lucrative in areas with a strong industrial sector or logistics hubs.

4. Multifamily Housing: Rental properties, such as apartments and condominiums, can provide a steady stream of income. Look for markets with a growing population and high demand for housing.

5. Specialty Properties: Depending on the market, specialty properties like hotels, medical facilities, or self-storage facilities can offer unique investment opportunities.

Remember, thorough research and due diligence are essential when identifying profitable real estate markets and property types. Stay informed, analyze market data, and seek advice from experienced professionals to make well-informed investment decisions.

When it comes to investing in commercial real estate, analyzing deals and evaluating potential returns is crucial for achieving profitable outcomes. As a beginner investor, it's important to develop a systematic approach to analyzing real estate deals to ensure you make informed decisions. Here are some key steps to consider:

**1. Identify Your Investment Criteria:**

Before diving into any deal, it's essential to identify your investment criteria. This involves determining your objectives, risk tolerance, and desired return on investment (ROI). By having clear criteria in mind, you can narrow down your search and focus on properties that align with your goals.

**2. Gather Relevant Property Information:**

Once you have identified potential properties, gather all the relevant information about each one. This may include property size, location, current and potential rental income, expenses, and vacancy rates. Conduct thorough research and ensure that the property meets your investment criteria.

**3. Analyze the Financials:**

Next, it's time to analyze the financials of the deal. Calculate key metrics such as the net operating income (NOI), cash flow, cap rate, and return on investment. These metrics will give you a clear picture of the property's profitability and help you compare different investment opportunities.

**4. Consider Market Factors:**

Don't forget to consider market factors when evaluating a potential real estate deal. Look at trends in the local market, such as population growth, job opportunities, and development plans. A strong market can contribute to the success of your investment, while a declining market may pose risks.

**5. Assess Risks and Mitigation Strategies:**

Every investment carries some level of risk, and it's essential to assess and mitigate these risks. Analyze potential risks associated with the property, such as tenant turnover, maintenance costs, or changes in zoning regulations. Develop strategies to minimize these risks and protect your investment.

**6. Seek Professional Advice:**

As a beginner investor, seeking professional advice can be

immensely beneficial. Consider consulting with real estate agents, property managers, or experienced investors who can provide insights and guidance. Their expertise can help you make more informed decisions and increase your chances of finding profitable deals.

By following these steps and consistently analyzing real estate deals, you can evaluate potential returns and increase your chances of finding profitable opportunities. Remember, thorough research and careful analysis are key to successful commercial real estate investing.

Effective negotiation techniques are crucial when it comes to finding profitable real estate deals. As a beginner in commercial real estate investing, mastering these techniques will help you secure favorable terms and maximize your returns. Here are some key negotiation strategies to keep in mind:

1. **Do Your Homework:** Before entering into negotiations, gather as much information as possible about the property and the market. Research comparable sales, rental rates, vacancy rates, and any other relevant data. This will give you a solid understanding of the property's value and help you negotiate from a position of knowledge and confidence.

2. **Set Clear Goals:** Determine your objectives and priorities before beginning negotiations. Are you looking for a lower purchase price, favorable financing terms, or perhaps additional concessions? Having clear goals will guide your negotiation strategy and enable you to focus on what truly matters to you.

3. **Build Rapport:** Establishing a positive relationship with the other party can greatly enhance your negotiation outcomes. Be respectful, communicative, and try to find common ground. Building rapport can lead to a more collaborative and mutually beneficial negotiation process.

**4. Listen Actively:** Pay close attention to the other party's needs, concerns, and motivations. Actively listening will allow you to identify potential areas of compromise and tailor your negotiation approach accordingly. Showing empathy and understanding can help foster a more productive negotiation environment.

**5. Be Patient:** Negotiations can often be lengthy and involve multiple rounds of back-and-forth. It's important to remain patient and avoid rushing into decisions. Take the time to carefully analyze and consider each offer or counteroffer before responding. Patience can lead to better outcomes and prevent you from making hasty decisions that may not be in your best interest.

**6. Seek Win-Win Solutions:** Aim for a negotiation outcome where both parties feel satisfied with the terms. Look for creative solutions that address the interests of both sides. By focusing on win-win solutions, you can build long-term relationships and increase your chances of finding future profitable real estate deals.

**7. Be Prepared to Walk Away:** Sometimes, despite your best efforts, negotiations may reach an impasse. It's essential to know your limits and be prepared to walk away if the terms are not favorable or if the other party is unwilling to meet your objectives. Being willing to walk away can demonstrate your resolve and may even prompt the other party to reconsider their position.

By incorporating these effective negotiation techniques into your commercial real estate investing journey, you'll be well-equipped to find profitable real estate deals and secure favorable terms. Remember, practice makes perfect, so continue honing your negotiation skills and adapt them to different situations and scenarios.

Managing and mitigating risks is an essential aspect of successful commercial real estate investing. By being proactive in identifying and addressing potential risks, you can safeguard your investments and maximize your chances of finding profitable real estate deals. Here are some key strategies to help you manage and mitigate risks in commercial real estate investments:

**1. Conduct thorough due diligence:** Before investing in any commercial property, it is crucial to conduct comprehensive due diligence. This involves thoroughly analyzing the property's financials, market conditions, tenant leases, and any potential legal or environmental issues. By doing so, you can identify any potential risks or red flags that may impact the profitability of the investment.

**2. Diversify your portfolio:** Diversification is a fundamental risk management strategy in any investment portfolio, including commercial real estate. By spreading your investments across different property types, locations, and asset classes, you can reduce the impact of any potential downturns or fluctuations in a specific market. Diversification helps you mitigate the risk of relying too heavily on a single investment.

**3. Build a strong network:** Networking is crucial in commercial real estate investing. By connecting with experienced professionals, such as real estate agents, property managers, and other investors, you can tap into their knowledge and expertise. A strong network can provide valuable insights, help you identify potential risks, and offer support in managing your investments.

**4. Evaluate financing options:** Understanding and evaluating different financing options is essential for managing risk in commercial real estate investments. By carefully considering the terms and conditions of loans, interest rates, and potential refinancing options, you can mitigate the risk of high debt levels or unfavorable financing terms. It is advisable to work with a knowledgeable mortgage broker or financial advisor to ensure you make informed decisions.

**5. Regularly monitor and review investments:** Once you have made an investment, it is essential to regularly monitor and review its performance. Stay updated on market trends, tenant occupancy rates, and any changes in the local economy that may impact your investment. By actively managing and reviewing your investments, you can identify and address any potential risks or issues before they escalate.

**6. Consider partnering with experienced investors:** If you are new to commercial real estate investing, partnering with experienced investors can help mitigate risks. By pooling resources and knowledge, you can leverage their expertise and reduce the potential for costly mistakes. However, it is crucial to choose partners carefully and establish clear communication and decision-making processes to ensure a mutually beneficial partnership.

**7. Stay informed and adapt:** The commercial real estate market is dynamic, and risks can change over time. Stay informed about industry trends, regulatory changes, and market conditions. Continuously educate yourself through books, articles, and networking events to adapt your investment strategies and mitigate potential risks.

By implementing these strategies, you can effectively manage and mitigate risks in commercial real estate investments. Remember, investing in real estate involves inherent risks, and while these strategies can help reduce those risks, they cannot eliminate them entirely. Always consult with professionals and make informed decisions based on careful analysis and due diligence.

## Conclusion Introduction

Investing in commercial real estate can be a lucrative venture for beginners. Throughout this lesson, we have explored the importance of finding profitable real estate deals in order to achieve a higher return on investment. By applying the strategies and tips shared, you can increase your chances of success in this competitive market.

If you feel the need to reinforce your understanding or revisit any concepts, we encourage you to review this lesson. Take your time to absorb the information and ensure you have a clear understanding of the steps involved in finding profitable real estate deals.

Remember, this lesson is just one part of a comprehensive course on commercial real estate investing. We highly recommend exploring the other lessons in the course to further enhance your knowledge and skills in this field. Each lesson builds upon the previous ones, providing valuable insights and practical advice to help you succeed in your real estate investment journey.

By remaining diligent, staying informed, and utilizing the strategies discussed, you can position yourself as a successful investor in the world of commercial real estate. Good luck on your journey to finding profitable real estate deals and achieving a higher return on investment!

# 3

# Understanding Real Estate Market Trends

If you are serious in investing in real estate, commercial properties can offer a lucrative opportunity. However, diving into the world of commercial real estate without a proper understanding of the market trends can be overwhelming and risky.

This self-guided online lesson aims to provide you with the knowledge and tools to navigate the commercial real estate market with confidence. By understanding real estate market trends, you will be able to make informed decisions, identify profitable opportunities, and mitigate potential risks.

In this lesson, we will explore various aspects of commercial real estate investing, including:

- The importance of market research
- Identifying emerging markets
- Understanding supply and demand dynamics
- Analyzing economic indicators
- Assessing the impact of technology on the market

By the end of this lesson, you will have a solid foundation in understanding real estate market trends, enabling you to make strategic investment decisions and maximize your returns in the commercial real estate sector.

Now, let's get started on your journey to becoming a successful commercial real estate investor!

In order to successfully invest in commercial real estate, it is crucial to have a deep understanding of the real estate market trends. By analyzing these trends, you can make informed investment decisions and maximize your returns. In this section, we will provide you with an introduction to real estate market trends.

Real estate market trends refer to the patterns and changes in the property market over a period of time. These trends can include factors such as the overall state of the economy, interest rates, population growth, supply and demand dynamics, and various other factors that impact the value and performance of real estate assets.

One of the key aspects of understanding market trends is analyzing historical data. By looking at past market trends, you can identify recurring patterns, cycles, and fluctuations in property prices, rental rates, and vacancy rates. This analysis can help you predict future trends and make more accurate investment decisions.

Another important factor to consider when analyzing real estate market trends is the location. Different regions and cities may experience different market trends based on their local economy, job growth, infrastructure development, and other factors specific to that area. It is crucial to research and understand the local market conditions before making any investment decisions.

Additionally, staying up-to-date with current news and events that may impact the real estate market is essential. Changes in government policies, zoning regulations, or industry trends can significantly affect property values and investment opportunities. Regularly monitoring real estate news sources and attending industry events can help you stay informed and adapt your investment strategy accordingly.

Lastly, it is important to keep in mind that real estate market trends are constantly evolving. What may be a favorable trend today may change in the future. Therefore, it is crucial to continuously educate yourself, stay proactive, and adapt your investment strategy as market conditions change.

In the next section, we will delve deeper into specific real estate market trends and how to analyze them effectively. Understanding these trends will provide you with valuable insights and give you a competitive edge as a commercial real estate investor.

Understanding the factors that influence real estate market trends is crucial for anyone interested in investing in commercial real estate. By analyzing these factors, you can make informed decisions and adapt your investment strategies accordingly. Here are some key factors to consider:

1. Economic Conditions: The overall state of the economy plays a significant role in the real estate market. Factors such as GDP growth, employment rates, interest rates, and inflation can influence property values and demand. For example, during periods of economic growth, property values tend to rise, while during recessions, they may decline.

2. Demographics: The demographic profile of an area can impact real estate market trends. Factors such as population growth, age distribution, income levels, and household size

can influence the demand for different types of properties. Understanding the demographics of a specific location can help you identify investment opportunities that align with market demand.

3. Supply and Demand: The balance between supply and demand is a critical driver of real estate market trends. When there is high demand and limited supply, property prices tend to increase. Conversely, when there is an oversupply of properties and low demand, prices may decrease. Monitoring the supply and demand dynamics in a particular market can help you determine the potential for growth or decline.

4. Government Policies and Regulations: Government policies and regulations can have a significant impact on the real estate market. Factors such as zoning laws, tax incentives, housing regulations, and infrastructure development can influence property values and investment opportunities. Staying informed about governmental initiatives and changes in regulations can help you anticipate market trends.

5. Technology and Innovation: Technological advancements and innovation can also shape real estate market trends. For example, the rise of e-commerce has led to increased demand for warehouse and distribution centers, while advancements in remote work have influenced preferences for office spaces. Keeping abreast of technological trends can help you identify emerging sectors and investment prospects.

Remember, understanding these factors is just the first step. Regularly monitoring and analyzing market trends will allow you to make informed decisions and adapt your investment strategies to maximize returns. By staying informed and proactive, you can navigate the complexities of the real estate market and achieve your investment goals.

When it comes to investing in real estate, understanding market trends is essential for making informed decisions. By analyzing historical data and current market indicators, you can gain valuable insights into the direction of the real estate market. Here are some key steps to help you analyze market trends:

**1. Historical Data Analysis:** Start by examining historical data of the real estate market in your target area. Look for patterns and trends in property prices, rental rates, vacancy rates, and sales volumes over the past several years. This data can give you a sense of how the market has performed in the past and help you identify any cyclical patterns or seasonal fluctuations.

**2. Economic Indicators:** Pay attention to economic indicators that can influence the real estate market. Factors such as GDP growth, employment rates, interest rates, and inflation can have a significant impact on property values and demand. Keep an eye on these indicators to gauge the overall economic health of the region you are interested in investing in.

**3. Demographic Trends:** Consider the demographic trends in the area you are targeting. Look at population growth rates, age distribution, and income levels. These factors can affect the demand for real estate, especially in residential and retail sectors. Areas with growing populations and rising incomes are generally more favorable for real estate investments.

**4. Market Supply and Demand:** Analyze the supply and demand dynamics in the market. Look at the current inventory of available properties and compare it to the demand from buyers or tenants. A high demand and low supply scenario may indicate a seller's market, while a high supply and low demand scenario could indicate a buyer's market. Understanding the balance between supply and demand can help you determine the potential for appreciation or rental income.

**5. Local Regulations and Development Plans:** Research local regulations and development plans that may impact the real estate market. Zoning restrictions, building permits, and infrastructure projects can influence property values and market dynamics. Stay informed about any upcoming developments or changes in regulations that could affect your investment strategy.

By analyzing historical data and current market indicators, you can develop a comprehensive understanding of real estate market trends. This knowledge will empower you to make well-informed decisions and maximize your chances of success in commercial real estate investing.

In order to successfully invest in commercial real estate, it is essential to understand the current market trends. Identifying emerging trends and potential opportunities can help you make informed decisions and maximize your investment returns. Here are some key steps to help you stay updated on the real estate market:

**1. Research Local Market:** Start by researching the local real estate market where you plan to invest. Look for data on property values, rental rates, vacancy rates, and economic indicators. Understanding the current state of the market will give you valuable insights into potential opportunities.

**2. Follow Industry News:** Stay updated on the latest news and trends in the commercial real estate industry. Subscribe to industry publications, follow relevant websites and blogs, and join online forums where professionals share insights and analysis. This will help you stay ahead of the curve and identify emerging trends early on.

**3. Network with Professionals:** Building a strong network of real estate professionals is crucial for staying informed about market trends. Attend industry conferences, join local real estate associations, and connect with professionals in your area. Engaging in conversations with experts and peers will provide you with valuable insights and potential investment opportunities.

**4. Analyze Market Data:** Dive deep into market data and analyze historical trends. Look for patterns and identify areas that have shown consistent growth or potential for future development. Utilize tools and resources such as market reports, demographic data, and economic forecasts to make data-driven investment decisions.

**5. Monitor Economic Factors:** Keep an eye on economic factors that can influence the real estate market, such as interest rates, employment rates, and GDP growth. Understanding how these factors impact the market can help you predict future trends and identify investment opportunities.

**6. Consult Experts:** When in doubt, consult with experienced real estate professionals, such as brokers, appraisers, and property managers. They can provide valuable insights and guidance based on their expertise and experience in the local market.

By diligently following these steps and continuously monitoring the real estate market, you will be better equipped to identify emerging trends and potential investment opportunities. Remember, staying informed and being proactive are key to successful commercial real estate investing.

Understanding real estate market trends is crucial for making informed investment decisions. By analyzing market trends, you can identify opportunities and potential risks, allowing you to maximize your returns and minimize potential losses. Here are some key steps to apply your knowledge of market trends to your real estate investing strategy:

**1. Research and analyze local market data:**

Start by researching and analyzing local market data to gain a deeper understanding of the current state of the real estate market in your target area. Look for information on property prices, rental rates, vacancy rates, and inventory levels. This data can help you identify trends and patterns that may impact your investment decisions.

**2. Identify emerging neighborhoods:**

Pay attention to emerging neighborhoods that show signs of growth and development. Look for indicators such as new infrastructure projects, commercial developments, and increasing property values. These neighborhoods often present opportunities for future appreciation and rental demand, making them attractive investment prospects.

**3. Monitor supply and demand dynamics:**

Keep a close eye on supply and demand dynamics in the real estate market. Understanding the balance between available properties and buyer/renter demand can help you determine whether it is a buyer's market or a seller's market. In a buyer's market, there is more supply than demand, giving you negotiating power. In a seller's market, there is more demand than supply, potentially driving up property prices.

**4. Stay informed about economic factors:**

Economic factors such as interest rates, employment rates, and GDP growth can significantly impact the real estate market. Stay updated on economic news and trends to understand how they may influence your investment decisions. For example, low-interest rates can make borrowing cheaper, while a strong job market can increase rental demand.

### 5. Seek expert opinions:

Consider seeking expert opinions from real estate professionals, economists, and market analysts. Their insights can provide you with valuable perspectives on market trends and help you validate your own research and analysis. Attend industry conferences, read reports, and engage with professionals to stay up-to-date with the latest market trends.

By applying your knowledge of real estate market trends, you can make more informed investment decisions and increase your chances of success in the commercial real estate market.

## Conclusion: Achieving Your Goal of Understanding Real Estate Market Trends

Throughout this lesson on commercial real estate investing for beginners, we have emphasized the importance of understanding real estate market trends to make informed investment decisions. By gaining a deep understanding of the market and its fluctuations, you can position yourself for success and maximize your returns.

If you feel the need to reinforce your knowledge or revisit any concepts discussed in this lesson, we encourage you to review the material. Take your time to absorb the information and ensure that you have a solid grasp of real estate market trends.

Remember, this lesson is just one piece of the puzzle. We have designed a comprehensive course on commercial real estate investing that covers various aspects and topics to help you become a successful investor.

Make use of the other lessons in the course to further expand your knowledge and skills. Each lesson builds upon the previous ones, providing you with a well-rounded understanding of the commercial real estate industry.

Investing in real estate can be a lucrative endeavor, but it requires careful analysis and informed decision-making. By committing to understanding real estate market trends, you are setting yourself up for long-term success. Keep learning, stay informed, and make the most of your investment opportunities.

# 4

# Understand Commercial Real Estate Investing

The goal of this text-based self-guided online lesson is to help individuals like you, who are new to real estate investing, gain a solid understanding of commercial real estate investing. By the end of this lesson, you will have a clear grasp of the basics, enabling you to make informed decisions and take the first steps towards building a successful real estate investment portfolio.

Whether you're looking to invest in office buildings, retail spaces, industrial properties, or any other type of commercial real estate, this lesson will provide you with the fundamental knowledge and tools you need to get started.

## What to Expect

In this lesson, we have prepared detailed solutions and explanations to help you achieve your goal. You will find step-by-step guides, practical tips, real-life examples, and resources to further expand your understanding of commercial real estate investing.

We have organized the lesson into easily digestible sections, covering topics such as market analysis, property evaluation, financing options, risk management, and more. Each section will build upon the previous one, gradually equipping you with the knowledge necessary to navigate the world of commercial real estate investing.

Remember, investing in real estate is a long-term commitment, and it's essential to approach it with the right knowledge and mindset. So, let's get started on your journey to becoming a confident commercial real estate investor!

Understanding the Real Estate Market

When it comes to investing in real estate, one of the key factors to consider is the real estate market itself. The real estate market refers to the overall conditions and trends in the buying, selling, and renting of properties in a specific area or region. Understanding the real estate market is crucial for making informed investment decisions that can maximize your returns and minimize risks.

One of the first things to grasp about the real estate market is the concept of supply and demand. Like any other market, the real estate market operates based on the principles of supply and demand. If there is high demand for properties in a particular area but limited supply, prices are likely to rise. On the other hand, if there is an oversupply of properties and low demand, prices may decline.

It's important to keep in mind that the real estate market is influenced by various factors, including economic conditions, population growth, employment rates, and interest rates. These factors can have a significant impact on property values and rental rates. For example, during periods of economic growth and low interest rates, the real estate market tends to thrive, leading to increased property values and rental income.

Another aspect of the real estate market to consider is market cycles. Real estate markets go through cycles of expansion, peak, contraction, and trough. Understanding these cycles can help you identify the best time to buy or sell properties. During the expansion phase, property prices are rising, making it an op-portune time to invest. However, during the contraction phase, prices may decline, presenting potential buying opportunities.

Additionally, it's essential to research and analyze the local market conditions before making any investment decisions. Factors such as neighborhood amenities, crime rates, school districts, and future development plans can all impact property values. By staying informed about the local market, you can identify emerging trends and areas that have the potential for growth.

Finally, keeping an eye on real estate market indicators can provide valuable insights into the overall health and direction of the market. Indicators such as average home prices, days on market, inventory levels, and rental vacancy rates can help you assess market conditions and make informed investment decisions.

Understanding the real estate market is a crucial step for beginners looking to invest in real estate. By studying supply and demand dynamics, considering market cycles, researching local market conditions, and monitoring market indicators, you can gain a better understanding of the real estate market and make informed investment choices.

One of the key aspects of successful commercial real estate investing is the ability to analyze investment opportunities effectively. By understanding how to analyze an investment opportunity, you can make informed decisions and increase your chances of achieving your financial goals. In this section, we will explore the fundamental steps involved in analyzing commercial real estate investment opportunities.

1. Market Research: Before diving into any specific investment opportunity, it is crucial to conduct thorough market research. This involves studying the current and projected trends in the local real estate market, analyzing supply and demand dynamics, and assessing the overall economic conditions of the area. By understanding the market, you can identify potential opportunities and make informed decisions.

2. Financial Analysis: Once you have identified a potential investment opportunity, the next step is to conduct a comprehensive financial analysis. This involves evaluating the property's income potential, assessing the expenses (including operating costs, taxes, and maintenance), and projecting the potential return on investment. By analyzing the financial aspects of the investment, you can determine whether it aligns with your investment goals and risk tolerance.

3. Due Diligence: Before making any investment, it is essential to perform due diligence. This involves conducting a thorough investigation of the property, including reviewing legal documents, inspecting the physical condition, and evaluating any existing leases or contracts. By conducting due diligence, you can uncover any potential issues or risks associated with the investment and make an informed decision.

4. Risk Assessment: Another critical aspect of analyzing investment opportunities is assessing the associated risks. This involves evaluating factors such as market volatility, competition, location-specific risks, and potential changes in the regulatory environment. By understanding and quantifying the risks involved, you can determine whether the potential returns

outweigh the risks and make an informed investment decision.

5. Exit Strategy: Lastly, it is essential to consider your exit strategy when analyzing investment opportunities. This involves determining how and when you plan to exit the investment, whether through selling the property, refinancing, or other strategies. Having a well-defined exit strategy can help you maximize your returns and mitigate potential risks.

By following these fundamental steps and conducting thorough analysis, you can increase your chances of identifying profitable commercial real estate investment opportunities. Remember, investing in real estate involves careful evaluation and decision-making, so take the time to analyze each opportunity before committing your capital.

When it comes to investing in real estate, one of the key considerations is financing. Understanding the various financing options available to you can help you make informed decisions and maximize your investment potential. Here, we will explore some common financing options for real estate investments.

1. Traditional Bank Loans: One of the most common ways to finance a real estate investment is through a traditional bank loan. These loans typically require a downpayment and are subject to interest rates and credit checks. Banks offer a variety of loan programs, including fixed-rate mortgages and adjustable-rate mortgages, allowing you to choose the option that best suits your needs.

2. Hard Money Loans: Hard money loans are short-term loans provided by private individuals or companies. These loans are typically used for fix-and-flip projects or when traditional financing is not readily available. Hard money loans often have higher interest rates and fees, but they can be obtained quickly, which is beneficial for time-sensitive investments.

3. Private Money Lenders: Private money lenders are individuals or groups who lend money to real estate investors. These lenders are not traditional financial institutions and may be more flexible in their lending criteria. Private money lenders often focus on the potential of the investment rather than the borrower's credit history.

4. Seller Financing: In some cases, the seller of a property may be willing to finance the purchase themselves. This is known as seller financing or owner financing. With this option, the buyer makes monthly payments directly to the seller instead of obtaining a traditional mortgage. Seller financing can be advantageous for both parties as it eliminates the need for a bank or lender.

5. Real Estate Investment Partnerships: Another financing option is to form a real estate investment partnership. This involves pooling resources with one or more investors to collectively purchase a property. Each partner contributes a portion of the purchase price and shares in the profits and risks of the investment. Real estate investment partnerships can be a great way to access larger deals and diversify your investment portfolio.

It's important to thoroughly research and understand the terms and conditions of each financing option before making a decision. Consider consulting with a financial advisor or real estate professional to help you navigate the various options and choose the one that aligns with your investment goals and risk tolerance.

Creating a Real Estate Investment Strategy is a crucial step in your journey to becoming a successful commercial real estate investor. A well-thought-out strategy will help you define your goals, assess risks, and make informed decisions. Here are some key steps to consider when creating your real estate investment strategy:

**1. Define Your Investment Goals:** Start by determining your investment objectives. Are you looking for long-term appreciation, regular cash flow, or a combination of both? Clarifying your goals will help you choose the right types of properties and investment strategies.

**2. Conduct Market Research:** Understand the local real estate market where you plan to invest. Analyze key factors such as population growth, employment rates, rental demand, and property values. This research will help you identify areas with potential for growth and profitability.

**3. Set a Budget:** Determine how much capital you are willing to invest and establish a budget for each property. Consider your financing options and calculate the expected returns on investment (ROI) to ensure your budget aligns with your goals.

**4. Diversify Your Portfolio:** Spread your investments across different property types and locations to minimize risks. Investing in a mix of residential, commercial, and industrial properties can provide stability and potential for higher returns.

**5. Assess Risk Tolerance:** Understand your risk tolerance level and factor it into your investment strategy. Real estate investments can come with risks such as market fluctuations, tenant turnover, and unexpected expenses. Determine how much risk you are comfortable with and adjust your strategy accordingly.

**6. Develop Exit Strategies:** Plan for the future by considering how you will exit your investments. Will you sell properties for profit, refinance to access equity, or hold them for long-term cash flow? Having a clear exit strategy will help guide your decision-making process.

**7. Stay Informed:** Real estate markets are constantly evolving, so it's important to stay up-to-date with industry trends. Follow real estate publications, attend industry events, and network with other investors to gain insights and make informed investment decisions.

By following these steps and continuously refining your real estate investment strategy, you will be well-prepared to navigate the world of commercial real estate investing and achieve your financial goals.

Managing and growing your real estate portfolio is a crucial aspect of successful commercial real estate investing. Once you have acquired your initial properties, it is important to have a solid plan in place to effectively manage and maximize the returns on your investments.

Here are some key strategies to consider:

## 1. Regular Property Maintenance

Regular maintenance is essential to preserve the value of your properties and ensure tenant satisfaction. Establish a schedule for routine inspections, repairs, and upgrades to address any issues promptly. This will not only keep your tenants happy but also help maintain the long-term value of your investment.

## 2. Effective Tenant Management

Tenant management is a critical aspect of real estate portfolio management. Develop a system for screening potential tenants, including background checks, credit checks, and verifying rental history. Establish clear and comprehensive lease agreements that outline tenant responsibilities and rent terms. Regularly communicate with your tenants and address any concerns or issues promptly to maintain good relationships and minimize turnover.

### 3. Financial Management

Proper financial management is essential for the growth of your real estate portfolio. Keep accurate and up-to-date records of income and expenses related to your properties. Set aside funds for regular maintenance, repairs, and unexpected expenses. Consider working with a professional accountant or property management software to help you track income, expenses, and cash flow effectively.

### 4. Continual Learning and Market Analysis

Real estate markets are constantly evolving, and staying informed about industry trends, market conditions, and investment opportunities is crucial. Dedicate time to research and attend industry events, webinars, and workshops to expand your knowledge. Regularly analyze your portfolio's performance and identify areas for improvement and potential growth.

### 5. Portfolio Diversification

Diversifying your real estate portfolio can help mitigate risks and maximize returns. Consider investing in different types of properties, such as residential, commercial, or industrial, in various locations. This will help spread your risk and provide opportunities for growth in different market segments.

By implementing these strategies, you can effectively manage and grow your real estate portfolio, increasing your chances of long-term success in commercial real estate investing.

## Conclusion

### *Keep Pursuing Your Real Estate Investing Goals*

As we come to the end of this lesson on commercial real estate investing for beginners, it's important to remind ourselves of the ultimate goal: to learn the basics of real estate investing and gain foundational knowledge. Investing in real estate can be a lucrative venture, but it requires a solid understanding of the fundamentals.

If you feel like you need to review any part of this lesson, take the time to do so. It's crucial to grasp the concepts and strategies presented here before moving forward. Remember, knowledge is power, and the more you learn, the better equipped you'll be to make informed investment decisions.

### *Make Use of the Other Lessons*

This lesson is just a small part of a larger course on real estate investing. If you found value in what you've learned so far, I encourage you to explore the other lessons in this course. Each lesson builds upon the previous one, taking you deeper into the world of real estate investing.

By taking advantage of the entire course, you'll gain a comprehensive understanding of commercial real estate investing. So, don't hesitate to continue your journey and expand your knowledge in this exciting field.

Remember, the goal is to equip yourself with the necessary

tools and knowledge to confidently invest in commercial real estate. So, keep learning, keep growing, and soon you'll be well on your way to achieving your real estate investment goals.

# 5

# Identifying Potential Risks

This lesson aims to provide you with essential knowledge and strategies to identify potential risks associated with investing in real estate.

Investing in commercial real estate can be a lucrative venture, but it also comes with its fair share of risks. Understanding and being able to identify these risks is crucial for making informed investment decisions and minimizing potential losses.

## Why Identifying Risks is Important

By learning to identify potential risks in real estate investing, you will be better equipped to evaluate investment opportunities and make informed decisions. Recognizing and understanding the risks involved allows you to develop risk mitigation strategies, safeguard your investments, and maximize your chances of success.

## What You Will Learn

In this lesson, we will cover various types of risks that are commonly associated with commercial real estate investing. We will explore factors such as market conditions, property-specific risks, financial risks, and legal considerations.

You will gain insights into the key indicators and warning signs that can help you assess and identify potential risks in your real estate investments. Additionally, we will provide practical tips and strategies to mitigate these risks and protect your investments.

## How to Use This Lesson

This self-guided online lesson is designed to be comprehensive and user-friendly. Each section will provide detailed information, examples, and real-world case studies to enhance your understanding of the risks associated with commercial real estate investing.

We encourage you to take your time, read through the material thoroughly, and make use of the provided solutions and resources. Feel free to bookmark this page for future reference and revisit any sections as needed.

Remember, successful real estate investing requires a combination of knowledge, analysis, and informed decision-making. Let's get started on our journey to identify potential risks in real estate investing!

In commercial real estate investing, it is important to understand the potential risks involved. By identifying these risks early on, you can make informed decisions and mitigate potential losses. Here are some types of risks commonly associated with commercial real estate investing:

1. Market Risk: This refers to the risk of fluctuations in the real estate market, including changes in property values, rental rates, and demand. Market risk can be influenced by factors such as economic conditions, interest rates, and local market trends. It is essential to research and analyze the market before making any investment decisions.

2. Financial Risk: Commercial real estate investments often require significant capital. Financial risk relates to the possibility of not being able to secure financing or meet financial obligations associated with the investment. It is crucial to have a solid financial plan in place, including a contingency fund to handle unexpected expenses.

3. Tenant Risk: Rental income is a significant component of commercial real estate investing. Tenant risk refers to the potential for tenants to default on their lease agreements or experience financial difficulties. Conducting thorough tenant screenings, including credit checks and rental history verification, can help mitigate this risk.

4. Operational Risk: Commercial properties require ongoing maintenance, repairs, and management. Operational risk involves the possibility of unforeseen maintenance issues, high vacancy rates, or difficulties in managing the property effectively. Conducting regular property inspections and having a contingency plan for property management can help reduce operational risks.

5. Legal and Regulatory Risk: Commercial real estate investing involves adherence to various laws, regulations, and zoning restrictions. Legal and regulatory risks include changes in zoning laws, environmental regulations, or potential lawsuits related to the property. Consulting with legal professionals

experienced in real estate can help identify and mitigate these risks.

6. Liquidity Risk: Commercial real estate investments are generally illiquid, meaning they cannot be quickly sold or converted into cash. Liquidity risk refers to the possibility of not being able to sell the property when desired or at the expected price. Understanding the market conditions and having a long-term investment strategy can help manage liquidity risk.

Remember, while there are risks associated with commercial real estate investing, there are also opportunities for substantial returns. By understanding and managing these risks, you can increase your chances of success in this investment avenue.

When investing in commercial real estate, it is crucial to identify and analyze potential market risks. Understanding these risks will help you make informed investment decisions and mitigate any potential negative impacts on your investment. In this section, we will explore some common market risks in real estate investing and provide you with strategies to manage them.

1. Economic Risks:

Market conditions play a significant role in the success of your real estate investment. Economic risks include factors such as inflation, interest rates, unemployment rates, and overall economic stability. A downturn in the economy can negatively impact property values and rental income. To mitigate economic risks, consider investing in diverse markets with a strong economic foundation and long-term growth potential.

2. Supply and Demand Risks:

Supply and demand imbalances can affect the profitability of your investment. An oversupply of commercial properties can lead to lower occupancy rates and reduced rental income.

Conversely, a high demand for properties can drive up prices, making it more challenging to find affordable investment opportunities. Thoroughly research the local market to understand the supply and demand dynamics before making an investment decision.

3. Regulatory and Legal Risks:

Regulatory and legal risks are essential to consider when investing in commercial real estate. Changes in zoning regulations, building codes, or environmental regulations can significantly impact your property's value and affect your ability to generate income. Stay informed about local laws and regulations and consult with legal professionals to ensure compliance and mitigate any potential legal risks.

4. Market Saturation Risks:

Market saturation occurs when there is an excessive supply of similar types of commercial properties in a specific location. This can lead to increased competition among property owners, resulting in lower rental rates and decreased cash flow. Before investing, evaluate the market for potential saturation and consider unique features or strategies that can differentiate your property from others in the area.

5. Tenant and Lease Risks:

The quality of tenants and the terms of the lease can pose risks to your investment. Non-payment of rent, lease disputes, or vacancies can impact your cash flow and overall profitability. Conduct thorough tenant screenings and ensure lease agreements are well-drafted, including provisions for potential risks such as late payments or lease termination. Regularly monitor tenant performance and address any issues promptly.

By identifying and analyzing these market risks, you can make informed investment decisions and develop strategies to mitigate any potential negative impacts. Remember to thoroughly research the market, consult with professionals, and stay updated on market conditions to ensure a successful commercial real estate investment.

When investing in commercial real estate, it is crucial to thoroughly evaluate property-specific risks before making any investment decisions. Understanding these risks will help you make informed choices and mitigate potential negative impacts on your investment.

1. Market Risk: One of the primary risks in real estate investing is market risk. This refers to the potential fluctuations in property values and rental rates due to changes in supply and demand dynamics, economic conditions, and market trends. Before investing, it is important to assess the overall health of the local real estate market and consider factors such as vacancy rates, rental growth, and market forecasts.

2. Location Risk: The location of a property plays a significant role in its investment potential. Factors such as proximity to amenities, transportation hubs, employment centers, and the overall desirability of the area can impact the property's long-term value and rental income. Evaluating the location risk involves conducting thorough market research and analyzing historical data to assess the stability and growth potential of the area.

3. Tenant Risk: Another critical factor to consider is the tenant risk associated with the property. This includes the creditworthiness and reliability of the tenants occupying the space. Assessing tenant risk involves conducting due diligence on existing tenants, evaluating their financial stability, lease terms, and occupancy rates. Understanding the tenant risk will help you gauge the stability of rental income and anticipate any

potential vacancies or lease defaults.

4. Physical Risk: Evaluating the physical condition of the property is essential in identifying potential risks. Conducting a thorough inspection, including structural, mechanical, and environmental assessments, will help you identify any existing or potential issues that may require significant repairs or renovations. Assessing physical risk will enable you to estimate the costs involved in maintaining and improving the property over time.

5. Regulatory and Legal Risk: Real estate investments are subject to various regulations and legal considerations. Understanding the zoning restrictions, building codes, environmental regulations, and lease agreements associated with the property is crucial to mitigate regulatory and legal risks. Conducting due diligence with the help of legal professionals can help you navigate any potential legal challenges or non-compliance issues.

By carefully evaluating property-specific risks, you can make informed decisions and develop strategies to minimize potential negative impacts on your commercial real estate investment. Conducting thorough research, seeking expert advice, and staying updated with market trends will enhance your ability to identify and manage these risks effectively.

In order to successfully invest in commercial real estate, it is crucial to assess and understand the potential financial risks involved. By proactively identifying and managing these risks, you can minimize potential losses and maximize your return on investment. Here are some key factors to consider when assessing financial risks in real estate investing:

**Market Volatility:** Real estate markets can be volatile, experiencing fluctuations in property values and rental rates. It is essential to analyze market trends, economic indicators, and local factors that may impact the demand and supply of commercial properties. Conduct thorough market research and consult with industry experts to gauge the stability and growth potential of the market you are considering.

**Financing Risks:** Securing financing for a real estate investment is often a significant challenge. Before committing to a property, thoroughly evaluate your financial capacity and the potential risks associated with obtaining a loan. Consider factors such as interest rates, loan terms, and the impact of changing market conditions on your ability to meet debt obligations.

**Property Management:** Effective property management is critical to the success of your investment. Consider the costs and risks associated with property management, such as maintenance expenses, tenant turnover, and potential legal issues. Hiring a reputable property management company or having a solid plan in place to handle these responsibilities can help mitigate these risks.

**Operational Costs:** Real estate investments come with various operational expenses that can impact your overall profitability. These costs may include property taxes, insurance, utilities, repairs, and vacancies. Thoroughly evaluate these expenses and factor them into your financial projections to ensure they align with your investment goals.

**Legal and Regulatory Risks:** Real estate investments are subject to a range of legal and regulatory requirements. Failure to comply with these obligations can lead to fines, legal disputes, or even loss of property. Engage with legal professionals who specialize in real estate to ensure you are aware of and comply with all relevant laws and regulations.

**Economic Downturns:** Economic downturns can significantly impact the real estate market and property values. Assess the potential impact of economic cycles on your investment and consider strategies to mitigate the risks associated with market downturns. Diversifying your portfolio, maintaining a strong cash reserve, and identifying properties with stable income streams can help safeguard your investment during challenging economic times.

**Exit Strategy:** Having a well-defined exit strategy is crucial when investing in commercial real estate. Market conditions and personal circumstances may change, requiring you to exit the investment earlier than anticipated. Consider potential exit strategies, such as selling the property, refinancing, or entering into joint ventures, to ensure you can exit the investment with minimal financial losses.

**Conclusion:** Assessing financial risks in real estate investing is a vital step in achieving long-term success. By thoroughly evaluating market volatility, financing risks, property management, operational costs, legal and regulatory risks, economic downturns, and having a well-defined exit strategy, you can make informed investment decisions and minimize potential financial losses.

In order to achieve success in commercial real estate investing, it is crucial to identify and mitigate potential risks associated with your investments. Implementing effective risk mitigation strategies can help protect your capital and maximize your returns. Here are some key strategies to consider:

**1. Conduct thorough due diligence:** Before investing in any commercial property, it is essential to conduct comprehensive due diligence. This involves thoroughly examining the property's financials, market conditions, legal issues, and potential risks. Hiring experienced professionals such as real estate attorneys, appraisers, and inspectors can provide valuable insights during this process.

**2. Diversify your portfolio:** Spreading your investments across different property types, locations, and markets can help mitigate risks. By diversifying your portfolio, you can reduce the impact of any negative events or fluctuations in a single property or market.

**3. Understand and manage financial risks:** Real estate investments carry financial risks such as interest rate fluctuations, rental income volatility, and unexpected expenses. It is important to have a thorough understanding of these risks and develop strategies to mitigate them. This may include setting aside contingency funds, securing long-term financing, and carefully analyzing rental income potential.

**4. Stay updated with market trends:** The real estate market is constantly evolving, and staying informed about current market trends is crucial for risk mitigation. Regularly monitor market conditions, vacancy rates, rental rates, and economic indicators to make informed investment decisions.

**5. Maintain adequate insurance coverage:** Adequate insurance coverage is essential to protect your investments from unforeseen events such as natural disasters, accidents, or lawsuits. Consult with insurance professionals to ensure you have the appropriate coverage for your real estate portfolio.

**6. Build a strong professional network:** Establishing relationships with industry professionals such as real estate agents, property managers, and contractors can provide valuable support in managing and mitigating risks. They can offer advice, insights, and recommendations based on their expertise and experience.

**7. Monitor and adapt:** Regularly monitor the performance

of your investments and be prepared to adapt your strategies if needed. Keep a close eye on market conditions, property maintenance, tenant satisfaction, and any potential risks that may arise. This proactive approach can help identify and address risks before they become significant issues.

By implementing these risk mitigation strategies, you can minimize potential risks and increase the likelihood of success in your commercial real estate investments. Remember, thorough research, careful planning, and ongoing monitoring are key to achieving your investment goals.

## Conclusion

In this lesson, we have explored the importance of identifying potential risks in real estate investing to minimize financial losses. As a beginner in commercial real estate investing, it is crucial to understand the potential risks associated with this type of investment.

### Remember Your Goal

Your goal is to achieve success in real estate investing by minimizing financial losses. By identifying potential risks, you can make informed decisions and take necessary precautions to protect your investment.

It is essential to recognize that real estate investing involves various risks, including market fluctuations, property damage, tenant issues, and legal complexities. By acknowledging these risks, you can develop strategies to mitigate them and enhance your chances of profitability.

## Review and Utilize

If you feel the need to reinforce your understanding or revisit any concepts covered in this lesson, don't hesitate to go back and review the material. It's always beneficial to refresh your knowledge and ensure you have a solid grasp of the subject matter.

Additionally, remember that this lesson is part of a comprehensive course on commercial real estate investing for beginners. The other lessons in the course cover various aspects of real estate investing, including property selection, financing options, and property management. Feel free to explore these lessons to broaden your knowledge and enhance your investment skills.

In conclusion, by identifying potential risks in real estate investing, you can minimize financial losses and increase your chances of success. Remember to review this lesson and make use of the other lessons in the course to further your understanding of commercial real estate investing. Good luck on your journey to becoming a successful real estate investor!

# 6

# Build a Strong Real Estate Investment Portfolio

The goal of this lesson is to help you build a strong real estate investment portfolio, specifically focusing on commercial properties. Investing in commercial real estate can provide a multitude of benefits, including secure cash flow, long-term appreciation, and diversification.

By the end of this lesson, you will have a clear understanding of the fundamentals of commercial real estate investing and be equipped with the strategies and techniques to make informed investment decisions. Whether you aspire to become a full-time real estate investor or simply want to enhance your investment portfolio, this lesson will give you the necessary tools to achieve your goals.

This lesson is designed to be self-guided, allowing you to learn at your own pace and revisit specific topics as needed. It contains detailed solutions and practical examples to help you better grasp the concepts discussed. So, let's get started on your journey to building a strong real estate investment portfolio!

Understanding the Basics of Commercial Real Estate Investing

Commercial real estate investing can be a highly lucrative venture, but it requires a solid understanding of the basics to build a strong investment portfolio. Here are some key concepts to grasp when starting out:

1. **Property Types:** Commercial real estate encompasses various property types, including office buildings, retail spaces, industrial properties, and multi-family residential buildings. Each type has its own unique characteristics and considerations, so it's crucial to familiarize yourself with the different options available.

2. **Market Analysis:** Conducting thorough market analysis is crucial to identify promising investment opportunities. This involves researching factors such as local economic conditions, population growth, vacancy rates, rental demand, and competition. A comprehensive understanding of the market will help you make informed investment decisions.

3. **Financial Analysis:** Analyzing the financial aspects of a potential investment is essential. This includes evaluating the property's income potential, operating expenses, cash flow projections, and potential return on investment (ROI). Understanding key financial metrics such as cap rates, net operating income (NOI), and cash-on-cash returns will enable you to assess the profitability of a property.

4. **Risk Assessment:** Real estate investing involves inherent risks, and it's crucial to assess and manage them effectively. Consider factors such as market volatility, tenant turnover, potential regulatory changes, and financing risks. Conducting thorough due diligence and working with experienced professionals can help mitigate risks and protect your investment.

5. **Financing Options:** Understanding the various financing options available for commercial real estate investing is

essential. These may include traditional bank loans, private equity, crowdfunding, or seller financing. Each option has its own advantages and considerations, so it's important to explore the most suitable financing strategy for your investment goals.

6. **Legal and Regulatory Considerations:** Commercial real estate investing involves navigating complex legal and regulatory frameworks. Familiarize yourself with zoning regulations, building codes, lease agreements, and any applicable tax laws. Consulting with legal professionals who specialize in commercial real estate can help ensure compliance and protect your investment.

By understanding these fundamental concepts of commercial real estate investing, you'll be better equipped to make informed decisions and build a strong investment portfolio. Remember to continue learning and staying updated with industry trends to maximize your potential for success.

Identifying and analyzing potential investment opportunities is a crucial step in building a strong real estate investment portfolio. By carefully evaluating properties and markets, you can increase your chances of making profitable investments. In this section, we will guide you through the process of identifying and analyzing potential investment opportunities.

The first step in this process is to define your investment criteria. This includes determining your investment goals, risk tolerance, and preferred property types. By clearly defining your criteria, you can narrow down your search and focus on opportunities that align with your objectives.

Once you have established your investment criteria, the next step is to conduct thorough market research. This involves analyzing local market trends, demographics, and economic indicators. By understanding the current and future potential of a market, you can identify areas with high growth potential and strong rental demand.

After analyzing the market, it's time to start searching for potential investment properties. There are several ways to find opportunities, including online listings, real estate agents, and networking with other investors. It's important to cast a wide net and explore various channels to increase your chances of finding the right property.

When evaluating potential investment properties, it's essential to conduct a detailed financial analysis. This includes assessing the property's income potential, expenses, and projected cash flow. Additionally, you should consider factors such as property condition, location, and potential for appreciation.

One useful tool for analyzing investment properties is the capitalization rate, or cap rate. The cap rate is calculated by dividing the property's net operating income by its purchase price. It provides a measure of the property's return on investment and allows for easy comparison with other properties.

Finally, it's crucial to perform thorough due diligence before making an investment decision. This involves conducting property inspections, reviewing financial documents, and verifying any potential risks or liabilities. By taking the time to gather all necessary information, you can make informed investment choices and mitigate potential risks.

In conclusion, identifying and analyzing potential investment opportunities is a vital step in building a strong real estate investment portfolio. By defining your investment criteria, conducting market research, and thoroughly evaluating properties, you can increase your chances of finding profitable investments. Remember to always perform due diligence and consider professional advice when making investment decisions.

Welcome to the section on evaluating risk and return in commercial real estate investments. In order to build a strong real estate investment portfolio, it is crucial to understand the risks involved and to assess the potential returns of your investments. By carefully evaluating these factors, you can make informed decisions that will help you achieve your investment goals.

When it comes to evaluating risk, there are several key factors to consider. One of the most important is the location of the property. Research the area's economic stability, population growth, and demand for commercial real estate. A property in a thriving market with strong demand is generally considered less risky than one in a declining market.

Another critical factor is the property's condition and potential for appreciation. Conduct a thorough inspection to identify any maintenance or structural issues that may require costly repairs. Additionally, analyze the property's historical and projected appreciation rates to assess its potential for long-term growth.

Furthermore, it is essential to evaluate the financial stability of potential tenants or lessees. A strong and reliable tenant can provide a steady income stream, reducing the risk of vacancy and missed rental payments. Consider the tenant's creditworthiness, lease terms, and industry stability before making your investment decision.

Now, let's turn our attention to assessing potential returns. One common metric used in commercial real estate investing is the capitalization rate, or cap rate. This ratio is calculated by dividing the property's net operating income (NOI) by its purchase price. The cap rate provides an indication of the property's potential return on investment, with higher cap rates generally indicating higher potential returns.

Additionally, consider the potential for rental income growth over time. Analyze the market trends and demand for commercial space in the area to determine if rental rates are likely to increase. This can contribute to higher cash flow and overall returns on your investment.

Lastly, take into account any tax benefits and incentives that may be available for commercial real estate investments. Consult with a tax professional to understand how depreciation, deductions, and other tax strategies can impact your overall returns.

By thoroughly evaluating the risks and potential returns of commercial real estate investments, you can make informed decisions that will help you build a strong real estate investment portfolio. Take the time to research and analyze each investment opportunity, considering factors such as location, property condition, tenant stability, cap rate, rental income growth, and tax benefits. With a well-balanced portfolio, you can maximize your returns and achieve your investment goals.

Building a strong real estate investment portfolio is essential for long-term success in commercial real estate investing. A well-diversified portfolio can help mitigate risks and maximize returns. Here are some key steps to consider when building your real estate investment portfolio:

**1. Set Clear Investment Goals:** Before you start investing, it's crucial to define your investment goals. Are you looking for steady cash flow, long-term appreciation, or a combination of both? Determine your risk tolerance and time horizon to align your investments with your objectives.

**2. Research and Analyze Markets:** Conduct thorough market research to identify areas with strong growth potential, favorable economic conditions, and increasing demand for commercial properties. Look for emerging markets or areas undergoing revitalization that offer attractive investment opportunities.

**3. Identify Your Investment Strategy:** Consider different investment strategies such as value-add, income-generating, or development projects. Each strategy has its own benefits and risks. Choose a strategy that aligns with your goals, expertise, and financial capabilities.

**4. Evaluate Properties Carefully:** When evaluating potential properties, conduct comprehensive due diligence. Consider factors like location, property condition, rental potential, zoning regulations, and market comparables. Seek professional advice from real estate agents, appraisers, and inspectors to make informed decisions.

**5. Diversify Your Portfolio:** Diversification is essential to reduce risks associated with real estate investing. Invest in a mix of property types, locations, and investment strategies to spread your risk. This can include residential, commercial, industrial, or even niche sectors like healthcare or self-storage.

**6. Manage Cash Flow Effectively:** Cash flow is the lifeblood of any real estate investment portfolio. Ensure you have a solid plan for rental income, expenses, and reserves. Regularly monitor your cash flow to optimize returns and address any issues promptly.

**7. Continuously Educate Yourself:** The real estate market is constantly evolving. Stay updated with industry trends, regulations, and market conditions. Attend seminars, read books, and network with other investors to expand your knowledge and make informed decisions.

**8. Regularly Review and Adjust:** Periodically review your investment portfolio to assess performance, identify areas for improvement, and make necessary adjustments. Stay agile and adapt your strategy as market conditions change to optimize your returns.

By following these steps and staying disciplined, you can build a strong real estate investment portfolio that generates consistent returns and helps you achieve your financial goals. Remember, real estate investing is a long-term journey, so patience and persistence are key.

One key aspect of building a strong real estate investment portfolio is diversifying your investment holdings. By diversifying, you spread your risk across different types of properties, locations, and tenants, which can help protect your investments from market fluctuations and unforeseen events.

Here are some strategies to consider when diversifying your commercial real estate investment portfolio:

**1. Property Types:** Investing in a mix of property types can help mitigate risk. Consider including office buildings, retail spaces, industrial properties, and multi-family units in your portfolio. Each property type has different demand cycles and can perform differently in various economic conditions.

**2. Geographical Locations:** Investing in properties located in different geographical areas can help protect your portfolio from localized economic downturns. Diversifying across different cities or regions can ensure that your investments are not solely dependent on the performance of one market.

**3. Tenant Diversity:** A diverse tenant mix can provide stability to your portfolio. Having a range of tenants from various industries and sectors can help reduce the risk of vacancy and ensure a steady income stream. Consider investing in properties with a mix of long-term leases and shorter-term leases to balance stability and flexibility.

**4. Investment Strategies:** Diversify your investment strategies by considering different approaches such as value-add properties, core properties, and opportunistic investments. Each strategy comes with its own risk-reward profile and can provide different income streams and potential for appreciation.

**5. Risk Tolerance:** Assess your risk tolerance and adjust your portfolio accordingly. If you have a lower risk tolerance, focus on more stable and income-generating properties. If you are comfortable with higher risk, consider adding properties with potential for higher returns but also higher volatility.

**6. Portfolio Size:** As your portfolio grows, ensure that you continue to diversify your holdings. Avoid concentrating too much of your investment in a single property or market. Regularly review your portfolio and rebalance if necessary to maintain a diversified approach.

Remember, diversification is a powerful tool in managing risk and maximizing returns in commercial real estate investing. By spreading your investments across different property types, locations, tenants, and strategies, you can build a strong and resilient real estate investment portfolio.

## Conclusion

Throughout this lesson on commercial real estate investing for beginners, we have explored the various aspects of building a strong real estate investment portfolio. Our main goal has been to emphasize the importance of diversifying investment holdings to achieve long-term success.

## *Review and Utilize*

If you feel the need to refresh your understanding or revisit any concepts covered in this lesson, we encourage you to review the material at your own pace. Taking the time to fully comprehend the content will greatly benefit your future investment decisions.

Additionally, remember that this lesson is part of a comprehensive course on commercial real estate investing. We recommend exploring the other lessons in the course to gain a well-rounded understanding of the subject matter.

By applying the knowledge gained from this lesson and the rest of the course, you will be better equipped to navigate the complexities of the real estate market and make informed investment choices.

Remember, building a strong real estate investment portfolio takes time and dedication. Stay committed to your goals and continuously seek opportunities to diversify your holdings. With patience and persistence, you can create a successful real estate investment strategy that aligns with your financial objectives.

# 7

# Secure Financing for Real Estate Investments

The goal of this self-guided online lesson is to provide you with detailed solutions and strategies to help you secure financing for your commercial real estate investments. Whether you are looking to purchase a retail space, office building, or industrial property, understanding the financing options available to you is crucial for success.

In this lesson, we will cover various topics such as:

- Types of financing available for commercial real estate investments
- Understanding loan terms and interest rates
- Building a strong credit profile for better financing options
- Working with lenders and understanding their requirements
- Creating a solid business plan to attract investors or lenders
- Exploring alternative financing options

By the end of this lesson, you will have a comprehensive understanding of the financing process for commercial real estate investments. You will be equipped with the knowledge and tools to confidently approach lenders, negotiate terms, and secure the financing you need to start or expand your real estate portfolio.

So, if you're ready to dive into the world of commercial real estate investing and learn how to secure financing for your investments, let's get started!

Understanding the Basics of Commercial Real Estate Financing is crucial for anyone interested in investing in real estate. Securing financing for your real estate investments can be a complex process, but with the right knowledge and preparation, you can increase your chances of obtaining the necessary funds.

When it comes to commercial real estate financing, there are several key factors to consider. The first is your creditworthiness. Lenders will review your credit score, credit history, and financial standing to assess your ability to repay the loan. It's important to maintain a good credit score and address any issues that may negatively impact your creditworthiness.

Additionally, lenders will evaluate the property itself. They will consider the property's value, income potential, location, and market conditions. It's essential to conduct thorough research and due diligence on the property to demonstrate its profitability and potential for long-term success.

Another crucial aspect of commercial real estate financing is the loan-to-value ratio (LTV). This ratio represents the percentage of the property's value that the lender is willing to finance. Generally, lenders prefer lower LTV ratios, as they provide a greater margin of safety for the loan and mitigate their risk. A lower LTV ratio may also result in more favorable terms and interest rates.

Furthermore, lenders will assess your ability to make a down payment. While residential real estate may require a down payment of around 20%, commercial real estate financing typically requires a higher down payment. It's important to have sufficient capital or access to funds to meet the down payment requirements.

Lastly, understanding the different types of commercial real estate financing options available is essential. These options include traditional bank loans, commercial mortgage-backed securities (CMBS), private lenders, and Small Business Administration (SBA) loans. Each option has its own requirements, terms, and interest rates. Researching and comparing these options will help you identify the best fit for your investment goals.

In conclusion, understanding the basics of commercial real estate financing is crucial for securing the necessary funds for your real estate investments. By focusing on your creditworthiness, property evaluation, LTV ratio, down payment capability, and exploring the various financing options, you can increase your chances of obtaining secure financing for your commercial real estate investments.

When it comes to securing financing for your real estate investments, one of the most important steps is preparing the necessary financial documents for loan applications. Lenders will require these documents to assess your financial stability and determine whether you are a suitable candidate for a loan. Follow these steps to ensure you are properly prepared:

**1. Personal financial statement:** This document provides an overview of your personal assets, liabilities, and net worth. It helps lenders evaluate your financial position and determine your ability to repay the loan. Include information on your savings, investments, real estate holdings, and any outstanding debts.

**2. Tax returns:** Lenders typically require the past two to three years of personal and business tax returns. This allows them to assess your income, deductions, and overall financial health. Make sure to include all schedules and attachments as requested by the lender.

**3. Bank statements:** Provide copies of your bank statements for the past six months to a year. Lenders want to see your cash flow, savings, and transaction history to gauge your financial stability. Organize the statements in chronological order and highlight any large deposits or withdrawals.

**4. Credit report:** Obtain a copy of your credit report from all three major credit bureaus: Experian, Equifax, and TransUnion. Review the report for any errors or discrepancies that could negatively impact your credit score. Address any issues before submitting your loan application.

**5. Business financial statements (if applicable):** If you are investing in real estate through a business entity, such as a limited liability company (LLC), provide the business financial statements. This includes profit and loss statements, balance sheets, and cash flow statements. These documents help lenders assess the financial health of your business.

**6. Rent roll and lease agreements:** If you are purchasing a property with existing tenants, include a rent roll that outlines the current rent amounts, lease terms, and expiration dates. Lenders will consider this information when evaluating the income potential of the property.

**7. Property appraisal:** Some lenders require a professional property appraisal to determine the market value of the property. This helps them assess the loan-to-value ratio and the overall risk associated with the investment.

**8. Projected financials:** Provide a detailed financial projection for the property, including income and expense estimates. This demonstrates your understanding of the investment's potential profitability and helps lenders assess the viability of the project.

By gathering and organizing these financial documents, you will be well-prepared to submit a loan application for your real estate investment. Remember to keep copies of all documents for your records and be thorough in your presentation to increase your chances of securing financing.

When it comes to investing in commercial real estate, securing financing is a crucial step in achieving your investment goals. There are various financing options available to investors, each with its own advantages and considerations. In this section, we will explore different financing options for commercial real estate investments.

1. Traditional Bank Loans: One of the most common financing options is obtaining a loan from a traditional bank. These loans typically have lower interest rates and longer repayment terms, making them suitable for long-term investments. To secure a bank loan, you will need to have a good credit score, a solid business plan, and collateral to offer as security.

2. SBA Loans: The Small Business Administration (SBA) offers loans specifically designed for small businesses, including those interested in commercial real estate investing. SBA loans often have more flexible requirements and lower down payment options, making them attractive to first-time investors. However, the application process can be more time-consuming.

3. Private Lenders: Private lenders, such as individuals or private investment firms, can provide financing for commercial real estate investments. These lenders may offer more flexibility in terms of eligibility criteria and loan terms. However, interest rates may be higher compared to traditional bank loans.

4. Crowdfunding: Another financing option gaining popularity in recent years is real estate crowdfunding. This involves pooling funds from multiple investors to finance a real estate project. Crowdfunding platforms enable investors to contribute smaller amounts, making it accessible to a broader range of investors. However, it's important to thoroughly research and evaluate the credibility and track record of the crowdfunding platform before investing.

5. Seller Financing: In some cases, sellers may be open to providing financing to buyers. This option can be advantageous for investors who may not qualify for traditional loans or who want to negotiate more favorable terms. However, seller financing options may come with higher interest rates and shorter repayment periods.

6. Hard Money Loans: Hard money loans are often used for short-term real estate investments, such as fix-and-flip projects. These loans are typically provided by private investors or companies and are secured by the property itself. Hard money loans have higher interest rates and shorter repayment terms, but they offer quick access to funds and more flexibility in terms of eligibility requirements.

Before deciding on a financing option, it's crucial to assess your financial situation, investment goals, and risk tolerance. Consider consulting with a financial advisor or real estate professional to determine the most suitable financing option for your commercial real estate investment.

When it comes to investing in commercial real estate, securing financing is a crucial step that can make or break your investment. Navigating the loan application process may seem daunting at first, but with the right knowledge and preparation, you can increase your chances of obtaining the financing you need. Here are some key steps to help you navigate the loan application process:

**1. Determine your financial goals:** Before approaching lenders, it's important to have a clear understanding of your financial goals. Consider factors such as your desired return on investment, cash flow requirements, and risk tolerance. This will help you determine the type and amount of financing you need.

**2. Gather necessary documentation:** Lenders will require various documents to assess your financial standing and evaluate the risk associated with lending to you. Some common documents you may need to provide include:

- Personal and business tax returns
- Financial statements (balance sheet, income statement, cash flow statement)
- Bank statements
- Property appraisal reports
- Lease agreements (if applicable)

**3. Improve your creditworthiness:** A strong credit history and score can significantly increase your chances of securing favorable financing terms. Take steps to improve your creditworthiness, such as paying off existing debts, maintaining a low credit utilization ratio, and correcting any errors on your credit report.

**4. Research and compare lenders:** Not all lenders are created equal, and it's important to find the right fit for your investment needs. Research different lenders, including traditional banks, credit unions, and online lenders, and compare their loan terms, interest rates, fees, and customer reviews. Choose a lender that aligns with your financial goals and offers competitive financing options.

**5. Prepare a comprehensive loan application:** A well-prepared loan application can significantly increase your chances of approval. Provide detailed information about your investment property, including its location, size, condition, and potential income. Clearly outline your investment strategy, including your expected return on investment and exit plan. Make sure to include all required documentation and double-check for any errors or omissions.

**6. Be responsive and proactive:** Throughout the loan application process, be responsive to any requests or inquiries from the lender. Address any concerns promptly and provide any additional information or documentation they may require. Being proactive and demonstrating your commitment to the investment can help build trust and improve your chances of securing financing.

**7. Seek professional advice:** If you're new to commercial real estate investing or the loan application process, consider seeking professional advice from a real estate attorney or financial advisor. They can provide valuable guidance, help you navigate complex legal and financial aspects, and ensure you make informed decisions.

By following these steps and being diligent in your loan application process, you can increase your chances of securing financing for your commercial real estate investments. Remember, preparation, research, and attention to detail are key to achieving your investment goals.

Managing and improving credit is crucial when it comes to securing financing for real estate investments. Lenders assess your creditworthiness to determine the level of risk involved in lending you money. Therefore, it's essential to take proactive steps to manage and improve your credit score. Here are some strategies to help you achieve this:

1. Review your credit reports: Start by obtaining your credit reports from all three major credit bureaus - Equifax, Experian, and TransUnion. Carefully review each report for any errors or discrepancies. If you find any inaccuracies, dispute them and have them corrected promptly. Ensuring the accuracy of your credit reports is vital in maintaining a good credit score.

2. Pay bills on time: Consistently making timely payments is one of the most effective ways to build and maintain a good credit history. Set up automatic payments or reminders to ensure you don't miss any due dates. Late payments can significantly impact your credit score, so make it a priority to pay all bills promptly.

3. Reduce debt: High levels of debt can negatively affect your credit score. Develop a plan to pay down your debts, starting with high-interest credit cards or loans. Aim to keep your credit utilization ratio below 30%, which means using no more than 30% of your available credit. This demonstrates responsible credit management and can improve your creditworthiness in the eyes of lenders.

4. Avoid new credit applications: Opening multiple new credit accounts within a short period can raise concerns for lenders and potentially lower your credit score. Avoid unnecessary credit applications while you're in the process of securing financing for real estate investments. Focus on maintaining your existing credit accounts and building a positive payment history.

5. Lengthen credit history: The length of your credit history also plays a role in your creditworthiness. If you have a relatively short credit history, consider keeping older credit accounts open even if you no longer use them. This demonstrates a longer and more established credit history, which can positively impact

your credit score.

6. Seek professional guidance: If you're unsure about how to manage or improve your credit, consider seeking guidance from a credit counselor or financial advisor. They can provide personalized advice based on your specific financial situation and help you navigate the complexities of credit management.

By implementing these strategies and consistently managing your credit, you can improve your creditworthiness and increase your chances of securing financing for real estate investments. Remember, building good credit takes time and effort, so stay committed to your financial goals and make credit management a priority in your real estate investment journey.

## Summary: Achieving Secure Financing for Real Estate Investments

In this lesson on commercial real estate investing for beginners, we have discussed the importance of securing financing to gain access to the necessary funds for your real estate investments. It is crucial to understand that without secure financing, it can be challenging to achieve your investment goals in the real estate market.

### Review and Utilize the Lesson

If you need to refresh your memory or dive deeper into the concepts covered in this lesson, we encourage you to review the material. Take the time to go through the lesson again, making sure you grasp the key points and strategies discussed.

Additionally, make use of the other lessons in this course to further enhance your knowledge and understanding of commercial real estate investing. Each lesson builds upon the previous one, providing you with a comprehensive understanding of the subject matter.

## Take Action

Now that you understand the significance of secure financing, it's time to put your knowledge into action. Take the necessary steps to secure financing for your real estate investments, keeping in mind the strategies and tips highlighted throughout this lesson.

Remember, acquiring the right financing is a critical component of successful commercial real estate investing. By securing the necessary funds, you can position yourself for lucrative opportunities and maximize your potential returns.

So, go ahead and take control of your financial future in the real estate market. We wish you the best of luck on your journey to becoming a successful real estate investor!

# 8

# Develop a Real Estate Investment Strategy

One of the first steps in your journey as a commercial real estate investor is to develop a solid investment strategy. Having a clear plan in place will help you make informed decisions and maximize your chances of success.

In this lesson, we will guide you through the process of developing a real estate investment strategy tailored to your goals and risk tolerance. We will cover key aspects such as understanding market trends, identifying investment opportunities, conducting due diligence, and creating a financial plan.

By the end of this lesson, you will have a comprehensive real estate investment strategy that aligns with your objectives and sets you on the path to achieving financial growth through commercial real estate.

Whether you are a novice investor or have some experience in residential real estate, this lesson will provide you with the necessary knowledge and tools to confidently enter the world of commercial real estate investing.

So, let's get started on developing your real estate investment strategy and unlock the potential of commercial real estate as an investment avenue!

Welcome to the section on Understanding the Basics of Commercial Real Estate Investing. Developing a real estate investment strategy requires a solid understanding of the fundamental concepts in commercial real estate. In this section, we will cover key aspects that will help you make informed decisions and set the foundation for a successful investment journey.

1. Property Types:

Commercial real estate encompasses a wide range of property types, each with its own characteristics and investment opportunities. Familiarize yourself with the various property types, including office buildings, retail spaces, industrial properties, multi-family units, and more. Understanding the different property types will enable you to identify which aligns with your investment goals and risk tolerance.

2. Market Analysis:

Conducting thorough market analysis is crucial in commercial real estate investing. Assessing the local market conditions, such as vacancy rates, rental rates, and demand, will help you identify areas with growth potential and better investment opportunities. Stay informed about economic indicators, population trends, and any upcoming developments that may impact the market.

3. Financial Analysis:

Before investing in commercial real estate, it's important to analyze the financial aspects of the property. Evaluate key financial metrics such as net operating income (NOI), cash flow, cap rate, and return on investment (ROI). Understanding these metrics will enable you to determine the profitability and potential risks associated with a particular investment.

4. Risk Assessment:

Every investment carries a certain level of risk. When developing your real estate investment strategy, it's essential to assess and manage these risks effectively. Consider factors such as market volatility, tenant stability, property location, and financing options. Diversifying your portfolio across different properties or asset classes can help mitigate potential risks.

5. Financing Options:

Explore various financing options available for commercial real estate investments. Research traditional bank loans, private lenders, crowdfunding platforms, and partnerships. Understanding the financing options will allow you to evaluate the best fit for your investment strategy, considering factors such as interest rates, loan terms, and your financial capability.

By grasping these fundamental aspects of commercial real estate investing, you will be better equipped to develop a real estate investment strategy that aligns with your goals and maximizes your potential for success. In the next section, we will delve deeper into the process of identifying investment opportunities and conducting due diligence.

When it comes to commercial real estate investing, there are various types of investments that you can consider. It is important to evaluate these different types in order to develop a real estate investment strategy that aligns with your goals and risk tolerance.

1. Office Buildings: Investing in office buildings can be a lucrative opportunity, especially in prime locations with high demand. These properties are typically leased to businesses and can provide a stable income stream. Consider factors such as vacancy rates, lease terms, and the overall economic health of the area when evaluating office building investments.

2. Retail Properties: Retail properties include shopping centers, malls, and standalone retail buildings. These investments are driven by consumer spending and can provide a steady cash flow if leased to reputable tenants. Evaluate factors such as foot traffic, tenant mix, and lease terms when considering retail property investments.

3. Industrial Properties: Industrial properties encompass warehouses, distribution centers, and manufacturing facilities. Investing in industrial properties can offer long-term stability, as these properties are typically leased on longer-term contracts. Consider factors such as location, accessibility, and the demand for industrial space in the area when evaluating these investments.

4. Multifamily Properties: Multifamily properties, such as apartment buildings or condominium complexes, can be a strong investment option. Rental income from multiple units can provide a consistent cash flow. Evaluate factors such as location, rental demand, and property management when considering multifamily property investments.

5. Hospitality Properties: Investing in hospitality properties, such as hotels or resorts, can be more complex due to the cyclical nature of the industry. Evaluate factors such as location, market demand, and the reputation of the property when considering hospitality investments.

6. Mixed-Use Properties: Mixed-use properties combine different types of real estate, such as retail, office, and residential spaces, within a single development. These investments can offer diversification and multiple income streams. Evaluate factors such as tenant mix, location, and market demand when considering mixed-use property investments.

Remember, when evaluating different types of commercial

real estate investments, it is crucial to conduct thorough research, analyze market trends, and consider your own investment objectives. Developing a well-rounded real estate investment strategy will help you make informed decisions and increase your chances of success in the commercial real estate market.

Developing a real estate investment strategy is crucial for anyone interested in investing in commercial real estate. By having a well-defined strategy, you can maximize your chances of success and minimize potential risks. Here are some key steps to help you develop a solid real estate investment strategy:

**1. Define your investment goals:** Start by clearly defining your investment goals. What do you hope to achieve through real estate investing? Are you looking for long-term rental income, short-term gains through flipping properties, or a combination of both? Understanding your goals will help shape your strategy.

**2. Assess your risk tolerance:** Real estate investing, like any investment, comes with its own set of risks. It's important to assess your risk tolerance level and determine how much risk you are willing to take. This will help you determine the types of properties and investment strategies that align with your risk profile.

**3. Conduct market research:** Before diving into any investment, it's crucial to conduct thorough market research. This includes analyzing local real estate trends, vacancy rates, rental rates, and economic indicators. Understanding the market conditions will help you identify potential investment opportunities and make informed decisions.

**4. Determine your investment criteria:** Based on your goals and market research, establish a set of investment criteria. This includes factors such as property type, location, size, budget, and potential returns. Having clear investment criteria will help you narrow down your options and focus on properties that align with your strategy.

**5. Build a network:** Real estate investing is a collaborative endeavor. Building a network of professionals such as real estate agents, brokers, lawyers, and property managers can provide valuable insights and opportunities. Networking with other investors can also help you learn from their experiences and gain valuable advice.

**6. Create a financial plan:** Developing a financial plan is essential for any real estate investment strategy. This includes determining your budget, financing options, and projected cash flows. It's important to factor in expenses such as property maintenance, taxes, insurance, and potential vacancies. A solid financial plan will help you evaluate the viability and profitability of potential investments.

**7. Continuously educate yourself:** Real estate markets are constantly evolving, so it's essential to stay updated and educated. Attend seminars, workshops, and webinars related to commercial real estate investing. Read books, articles, and blogs by experts in the field. Continuously expanding your knowledge will help you adapt to market changes and make informed investment decisions.

By following these steps and developing a well-thought-out real estate investment strategy, you can increase your chances of success in commercial real estate investing. Remember, investing in real estate requires patience, diligence, and a long-term perspective. Take the time to develop a strategy that aligns with your goals and risk tolerance, and you'll be on your way to building a profitable real estate portfolio.

When developing a real estate investment strategy, it is essential to analyze the risks and returns associated with commercial real estate investing. Understanding the potential risks and returns will help you make informed decisions and maximize your investment's profitability.

1. Risks:

Commercial real estate investing involves certain risks that you need to be aware of before making any investment decisions. Some common risks include:

- Market Risk: The overall performance of the real estate market can affect the value and returns of your investment. Factors such as economic conditions, supply and demand, and interest rates can impact the market's stability.

- Property-Specific Risk: Each property has its own set of risks, including location, condition, and potential legal or environmental issues. It is crucial to thoroughly evaluate these risks before investing to mitigate any potential problems in the future.

- Tenant Risk: Commercial properties rely on tenants to generate rental income. The risk of tenant default or vacancy can impact your cash flow. Conducting thorough tenant screenings and maintaining strong lease agreements can help mitigate this risk.

2. Returns:

Commercial real estate investing offers various avenues for generating returns. Some key returns to consider include:

- Rental Income: The primary source of returns in commercial real estate investing comes from rental income. Analyze the current and potential rental rates in the market to estimate your cash flow and determine the property's income potential.

- Appreciation: Properties can appreciate in value over time, allowing you to benefit from capital appreciation. Analyze historical market trends and consider factors that can contribute to property value appreciation, such as location and development plans in the area.

- Tax Benefits: Real estate investments offer certain tax advantages, such as depreciation deductions and the ability to defer capital gains taxes through 1031 exchanges. Consult with a tax professional to understand how these benefits can impact your overall returns.

3. Risk-Return Tradeoff:

It is important to strike a balance between risks and returns when developing your real estate investment strategy. Higher returns often come with higher risks, so it is crucial to assess your risk tolerance and align it with your investment goals. Diversification across different property types and locations can help mitigate risks and optimize returns.

By thoroughly analyzing the risks and returns associated with commercial real estate investing, you can make informed decisions and develop a robust investment strategy. Remember to conduct thorough due diligence, seek professional advice when needed, and stay updated with market trends to ensure the success of your investment ventures.

Developing a real estate investment strategy is crucial for optimizing investment outcomes in commercial real estate. Without a well-defined strategy, investors may find themselves making haphazard decisions that can lead to missed opportunities and financial losses. In this section, we will explore key steps to help you develop an effective real estate investment strategy.

1. Define Your Investment Objectives:

Start by clearly defining your investment objectives. Are you looking for long-term capital appreciation, regular rental income, or a combination of both? Consider your risk tolerance, time horizon, and financial goals. This will help guide your decision-making process and determine the types of properties and markets you should focus on.

2. Conduct Market Research:

Thorough market research is essential for identifying promising investment opportunities. Analyze trends in the commercial real estate market, including vacancy rates, rental rates, and development activity. Pay attention to economic indicators and demographic data that can impact the demand and supply of commercial properties. This research will help you identify markets with strong growth potential.

3. Determine Your Investment Criteria:

Establish clear investment criteria based on your objectives and risk appetite. Consider factors such as property type (office, retail, industrial, etc.), location, size, and price range. Determine the minimum return on investment (ROI) you require and any specific financial metrics you want to achieve. Having these criteria in place will help you filter out properties that do not align with your investment strategy.

4. Build a Network of Professionals:

Real estate investing involves collaboration with various professionals, including real estate agents, attorneys, accountants, and property managers. Build a network of trustworthy professionals who can provide guidance and support throughout your investment journey. They can help you identify potential deals, negotiate contracts, conduct due diligence, and manage your properties effectively.

5. Evaluate Risk and Diversify:

Risk management is essential in any investment strategy. Evaluate the risks associated with commercial real estate investing, such as market fluctuations, tenant turnover, and regulatory changes. Consider diversifying your portfolio by investing in different property types, locations, and markets. This can help mitigate risk and maximize potential returns.

6. Continuously Monitor and Adjust:

Real estate markets are dynamic, and it's important to continuously monitor and evaluate your investment performance. Stay updated on market trends, rental rates, and property values. Regularly review your investment portfolio and make adjustments as needed to align with your evolving objectives and market conditions.

By following these steps and developing a well-thought-out real estate investment strategy, you can optimize your investment outcomes in commercial real estate. Remember to stay informed, seek professional advice when needed, and always conduct thorough due diligence before making any investment decisions.

## Summary

Throughout this lesson, we have explored the exciting world of commercial real estate investing for beginners. We have discussed the reasons why people are interested in investing in real estate and the potential benefits it can bring. Our focus has been on developing a real estate investment strategy to optimize investment outcomes.

### Importance of Developing a Real Estate Investment Strategy

Developing a real estate investment strategy is crucial for anyone looking to invest in this market. Without a well-thought-out plan, it can be easy to get overwhelmed and make decisions based on emotions or short-term trends. By taking the time to develop a strategy, you are setting yourself up for long-term success and maximizing your investment potential.

## Review and Utilize the Lessons

If you feel the need to review any part of this lesson, we encourage you to do so. Taking the time to revisit key concepts or strategies can help reinforce your understanding and ensure that you are on the right track. Additionally, don't forget to make use of the other lessons in this course. Each lesson builds upon the previous one, providing a comprehensive foundation for your real estate investment journey.

Remember, the goal is to develop a real estate investment strategy that aligns with your financial objectives and risk tolerance. By doing so, you can optimize your investment outcomes and increase your chances of long-term success in the world of commercial real estate investing.

# 9

# Navigating Legal and Regulatory Requirements

Whether you are a seasoned investor looking to diversify your portfolio or a newcomer interested in exploring the world of real estate, this lesson is designed to equip you with the knowledge and skills necessary to navigate the legal and regulatory requirements in commercial real estate investing.

## The Goal: Understanding Legal and Regulatory Requirements

Investing in commercial real estate can be a lucrative venture, but it also comes with its fair share of legal and regulatory complexities. Understanding and adhering to these requirements is crucial to ensure that your investments are compliant, protected, and successful.

In this lesson, our goal is to provide you with a comprehensive overview of the legal and regulatory landscape in commercial real estate investing. We will cover a wide range of topics, including property acquisition, leasing agreements, zoning laws, tax implications, and more.

## Why Navigating Legal and Regulatory Requirements is Important

By gaining a thorough understanding of the legal and regulatory requirements, you will be able to make informed decisions, mitigate risks, and maximize the potential returns on your investments. Navigating these requirements can be challenging, but with the right knowledge and guidance, you can confidently navigate the complex world of commercial real estate investing.

Throughout this lesson, we will provide you with detailed solutions and practical advice to help you overcome common legal and regulatory hurdles. Whether you are considering investing in office buildings, retail spaces, or industrial properties, this lesson will equip you with the necessary tools to navigate the legal landscape and make informed investment decisions.

So, let's dive in and start navigating the legal and regulatory requirements in commercial real estate investing!

Understanding the legal framework in real estate investing is crucial for beginners looking to navigate the legal and regulatory requirements of this industry. Real estate is subject to various laws and regulations at the local, state, and federal levels, which can significantly impact your investment decisions and strategies.

One of the most important legal aspects to consider is zoning and land use regulations. Zoning laws dictate how land can be used in a particular area, such as residential, commercial, or industrial. It is essential to understand the zoning regulations in the location where you plan to invest, as they can determine what type of property you can develop or purchase.

Additionally, you should familiarize yourself with building codes and permits. Building codes ensure that structures meet safety and health standards, and permits are required for construction or renovation projects. Violating these codes or proceeding without the necessary permits can lead to penalties and legal issues.

Another critical aspect of the legal framework is property ownership and title. Before investing, it is essential to conduct a thorough title search to ensure there are no liens, easements, or other encumbrances on the property. Understanding property ownership laws and rights can help protect your investment and avoid any potential disputes.

Furthermore, it is important to be aware of landlord-tenant laws if you plan to invest in rental properties. These laws govern the rights and responsibilities of landlords and tenants, including lease agreements, eviction processes, and maintenance obligations. Understanding these laws will help you manage your rental properties legally and avoid any legal disputes.

Lastly, it is highly recommended to consult with legal professionals, such as real estate attorneys, who specialize in the laws and regulations of the specific area where you plan to invest. They can provide valuable guidance and ensure that you navigate the legal framework successfully.

By understanding the legal framework in real estate investing, you can make informed decisions, mitigate risks, and ensure compliance with applicable laws and regulations. Take the time to educate yourself about the legal requirements and seek professional advice when needed to protect your investments and navigate the real estate market confidently.

When investing in commercial real estate, it is crucial to navigate the legal and regulatory requirements to ensure a successful and compliant investment. One important aspect to consider is zoning and land use regulations.

Zoning regulations dictate how a particular area can be used, such as residential, commercial, industrial, or mixed-use. These regulations are put in place by local government authorities to control and manage land development and ensure compatibility between different land uses.

Here are some steps to help you identify and comply with zoning and land use regulations:

**1. Research local zoning ordinances:** Start by researching the zoning ordinances specific to the area where you plan to invest. Most municipalities have zoning maps and codes available online or at local government offices. Familiarize yourself with the regulations applicable to your desired property type.

**2. Determine the zoning classification:** Once you have reviewed the zoning ordinances, identify the zoning classification of the property you are interested in. This classification will determine the allowable uses, such as residential, commercial, or industrial.

**3. Understand the restrictions and requirements:** Each zoning classification comes with its own set of restrictions and requirements. These may include building height limitations, parking space ratios, signage regulations, and more. Make sure you understand these restrictions and assess if they align with your investment goals.

**4. Seek professional guidance:** If you find the zoning regulations complex or need further clarification, it is advisable to consult with a real estate attorney or professional familiar with local zoning laws. They can provide valuable insights and ensure you remain compliant throughout the investment process.

**5. Apply for necessary permits:** If your investment plans

85

require a change in land use or building modifications, you may need to apply for permits from the local government. Ensure you follow the proper application process and obtain all necessary permits before proceeding with your investment.

By carefully navigating zoning and land use regulations, you can ensure that your commercial real estate investment meets all legal requirements and operates in harmony with the surrounding area. Compliance with these regulations is essential for a successful and sustainable investment journey.

One important aspect of navigating the legal and regulatory requirements in commercial real estate investing is understanding property tax laws and regulations. Property taxes are a significant financial obligation for real estate investors, and it is crucial to have a clear understanding of how they work to effectively manage your investments.

Here are some key points to consider when it comes to property tax laws and regulations:

**1. Assessment Process:** Property taxes are typically assessed by local government authorities based on the value of the property. It is important to understand how the assessment process works in your jurisdiction. Assessments can be based on the market value of the property or its income-generating potential, such as in the case of commercial properties.

**2. Exemptions and Incentives:** Some jurisdictions offer exemptions or incentives for certain types of properties or specific real estate investments. These exemptions can vary widely, so it is essential to research and understand the available options in your area. Examples may include tax breaks for historic properties or properties used for affordable housing.

**3. Appeal Process:** If you believe that your property has been assessed incorrectly or unfairly, you have the right to appeal the assessment. Familiarize yourself with the appeal process in your jurisdiction, including deadlines, required documentation, and any associated fees. It may be beneficial to consult with a real estate attorney or tax professional to navigate this process effectively.

**4. Tax Payment Schedule:** Property taxes are typically due at specific intervals, such as annually, semi-annually, or quarterly. Make sure you are aware of the payment schedule in your area and plan your finances accordingly. Failure to pay property taxes on time can result in penalties and interest charges.

**5. Tax Planning Strategies:** Property taxes can have a significant impact on your overall investment returns. Consider implementing tax planning strategies to minimize your tax liability legally. This may involve consulting with a tax professional who specializes in real estate to identify potential deductions, credits, or other tax-saving opportunities.

By understanding and navigating property tax laws and regulations, you can effectively manage this critical aspect of commercial real estate investing. Stay informed, seek professional advice when needed, and ensure compliance with all legal and regulatory requirements to protect your investments.

Ensuring compliance with building codes and permits is an essential aspect of real estate investing. Adhering to legal and regulatory requirements not only helps you avoid costly penalties but also ensures the safety and integrity of your property. Here are some key considerations to help you navigate building codes and permits:

**Research local building codes:** Each jurisdiction may have its own set of building codes and regulations that govern construction and renovation projects. It is crucial to research and familiarize yourself with the specific codes in the area where you plan to invest. These codes typically cover areas such as structural integrity, fire safety, electrical and plumbing systems, accessibility, and more.

**Consult with professionals:** Engaging with professionals such as architects, engineers, and contractors who are well-versed in local building codes can provide invaluable guidance. These experts can help you understand the specific requirements and guide you through the process of obtaining necessary permits and approvals.

**Obtain necessary permits:** Before starting any construction or renovation work, it is important to obtain the required permits from the local building department. These permits typically include building permits, electrical permits, plumbing permits, and more. Failing to obtain the necessary permits can result in fines, delays, and even forced removal of unauthorized work.

**Follow inspection procedures:** Building inspections are typically conducted at various stages of a construction project to ensure compliance with building codes and regulations. It is important to schedule and pass these inspections to demonstrate that your property meets the required standards. Inspections may cover areas such as structural components, electrical systems, plumbing, fire safety measures, and more.

**Maintain documentation:** It is essential to keep detailed records of all permits, inspections, and approvals obtained throughout the process. These records serve as proof of compliance and can be useful in the future when selling the property or during any potential audits. Make sure to organize and store these documents in a safe and easily accessible manner.

By prioritizing compliance with building codes and permits, you can ensure that your real estate investments meet legal requirements and are safe for occupants. Remember, each jurisdiction may have specific regulations, so thorough research and professional guidance are key to successfully navigating these legal and regulatory obligations.

When investing in commercial real estate, it is crucial to navigate the legal and regulatory requirements to avoid penalties and legal issues. Understanding and complying with these requirements will not only protect your investments but also ensure a smooth and successful real estate investing journey.

Here are some key steps to help you avoid penalties and legal issues:

1. Research and Understand Local Laws and Regulations:

Before starting your real estate investment journey, take the time to research and understand the local laws and regulations that govern commercial real estate. This includes zoning laws, building codes, permits, and any other requirements specific to your target area. Familiarize yourself with these regulations to ensure that your investment plans align with the legal requirements.

2. Consult with Professionals:

Seek the advice of professionals who specialize in commercial real estate investing, such as real estate attorneys, accountants, and property managers. These professionals can guide you through the legal and regulatory landscape, helping you make informed decisions and avoid potential pitfalls. Their expertise and knowledge will be invaluable in ensuring compliance with relevant laws and regulations.

3. Form a Legal Entity:

Consider forming a legal entity, such as a limited liability company (LLC), to protect your personal assets and minimize potential liability. This step can provide an additional layer of protection against legal issues that may arise during the course of your real estate investments. Consult with an attorney to determine the most suitable legal entity structure for your specific investment goals.

4. Obtain the Necessary Permits and Licenses:

Make sure to obtain all the necessary permits and licenses required for your commercial real estate investment. This may include permits for construction or renovation, business licenses, and any other permits specific to your property type or location. Failing to obtain the required permits can result in costly penalties and delays, so it's essential to complete this step before proceeding with your investment plans.

5. Comply with Fair Housing Laws:

When engaging in commercial real estate investing, it's important to understand and comply with fair housing laws. These laws prohibit discrimination based on race, color, religion, sex, national origin, disability, and familial status. Familiarize yourself with fair housing laws to ensure that your tenant selection process and property management practices align with these regulations.

By following these steps, you can navigate the legal and regulatory requirements of commercial real estate investing and avoid penalties and legal issues. Remember, it's always better to be proactive and informed when it comes to legal matters in the real estate industry.

## Conclusion

In this lesson, we have explored the importance of navigating legal and regulatory requirements when investing in commercial real estate. By ensuring compliance and avoiding penalties, you can protect your investments and maintain a strong financial position.

Remember, the legal and regulatory landscape can be complex and ever-changing. It is crucial to stay informed and updated on relevant laws, regulations, and requirements that pertain to real estate investing. This will help you make informed decisions and mitigate potential risks.

## Review and Utilize

If you feel the need to refresh your understanding of the material covered in this lesson, we encourage you to review it again. You can always access this lesson at any time to reinforce your knowledge and clarify any doubts.

Additionally, make use of the other lessons in this course to further enhance your understanding of commercial real estate investing. Each lesson covers various aspects and strategies that will equip you with the knowledge and skills needed to succeed in this field.

By consistently educating yourself and staying aware of legal and regulatory requirements, you are positioning yourself for success as a real estate investor. Good luck on your investing journey!

# 10

# Maximize Cash Flow

Whatever your situation may be, this self-guided online lesson is designed to help beginners like you understand the fundamentals of commercial real estate investing and, more importantly, how to maximize cash flow from your real estate investments.

Investing in commercial real estate can be a lucrative venture, but it requires a solid understanding of the market, thorough research, and strategic decision-making. This lesson will provide you with the knowledge and tools you need to make informed investment choices and increase the cash flow generated by your real estate properties.

By the end of this lesson, you will have a clear understanding of the key factors to consider when investing in commercial real estate, such as location, property types, financing options, and risk management. You will also learn practical strategies to maximize cash flow, including property valuation techniques, lease negotiation tactics, and property management best practices.

Whether you are interested in retail properties, office buildings, industrial spaces, or other commercial real estate opportunities, this lesson will equip you with the essential knowledge and skills to confidently navigate the world of commercial real estate investing.

So, let's get started and embark on this exciting journey to maximize cash flow from your real estate investments!

Understanding the Basics of Commercial Real Estate Investing

In order to maximize cash flow from your real estate investments, it is important to have a solid understanding of the basics of commercial real estate investing. This knowledge will help you make informed decisions and navigate the complexities of the market.

1. Types of Commercial Real Estate

Commercial real estate encompasses various types of properties, including office buildings, retail spaces, industrial properties, and multi-family residential buildings. Each type has its own unique characteristics and considerations. It is essential to familiarize yourself with the different types of commercial real estate to determine which sector aligns with your investment goals and risk tolerance.

2. Location and Market Analysis

Location is crucial when it comes to commercial real estate investing. Conduct thorough market research to identify areas with strong economic growth, low vacancy rates, and high demand for the type of property you intend to invest in. Analyze market trends, demographics, and local regulations to assess the long-term viability and potential profitability of a particular location.

3. Financial Analysis

Before investing in commercial real estate, it is essential to perform a comprehensive financial analysis. Calculate the potential return on investment (ROI), taking into account factors such as rental income, operating expenses, financing costs, and potential appreciation. Consider consulting with a financial advisor or real estate professional to ensure accurate and thorough analysis.

4. Risk Assessment and Mitigation

Commercial real estate investments come with inherent risks, such as market volatility, tenant turnover, and property maintenance. It is crucial to assess and mitigate these risks to protect your investment. Conduct due diligence on the property, review lease agreements, and consider obtaining insurance coverage to minimize potential losses.

5. Financing Options

Explore different financing options available for commercial real estate investing. These may include traditional bank loans, private lenders, or partnerships. Evaluate the terms, interest rates, and repayment schedules to determine the most suitable financing option for your investment strategy.

6. Network and Professional Support

Building a network of professionals in the commercial real estate industry can provide valuable guidance and support. Engage with real estate agents, property managers, attorneys, and other investors to gain insights and access to potential investment opportunities. Networking can also help you stay updated on industry trends and developments.

By understanding these basics of commercial real estate investing, you will be better equipped to make informed decisions and maximize cash flow from your real estate investments.

When it comes to commercial real estate investing, one of the key goals is to maximize cash flow from your investments. This means finding profitable opportunities that will generate consistent income for you over time. In this section, we will discuss how to identify these opportunities and make informed decisions.

The first step in identifying profitable commercial real estate opportunities is to research and analyze the market. Look for areas that are experiencing growth and have a high demand for commercial properties. This could be due to factors such as population growth, job opportunities, or the presence of major businesses in the area.

Next, consider the property type that will best suit your investment goals. Commercial real estate includes various types such as office buildings, retail spaces, industrial properties, and multi-family residential buildings. Each type comes with its own set of risks and rewards, so it's important to choose the one that aligns with your investment strategy and risk tolerance.

Once you have identified the property type, it's time to evaluate potential investment opportunities. Look for properties that have a strong potential for rental income. Consider factors such as location, accessibility, and amenities that will attract tenants and ensure high occupancy rates.

Additionally, analyze the financials of the property. Calculate the potential rental income, operating expenses, and any financing costs to determine the cash flow you can expect. It's crucial to conduct a thorough financial analysis to ensure that the property will generate positive cash flow and meet your investment objectives.

Furthermore, consider the potential for appreciation. While cash flow is important, the value of the property can also increase over time, resulting in a higher return on investment. Research the historical and projected growth in property values in the area to assess the appreciation potential of the investment.

Lastly, don't forget to conduct due diligence before finalizing any investment. This involves reviewing property documents, conducting property inspections, and evaluating any potential risks or legal issues. It's essential to have a clear understanding of the property's condition and any potential challenges it may present.

By following these steps and conducting thorough research and analysis, you can identify profitable commercial real estate opportunities that will help you maximize cash flow from your investments. Remember to stay informed about market trends and seek professional advice when needed to make informed investment decisions.

In order to maximize cash flow from your real estate investments, it is crucial to analyze the cash flow potential and return on investment (ROI) of each property. This will help you make informed decisions and ensure that you are investing in properties that will generate the desired income.

When analyzing the cash flow potential of a property, there are several key factors to consider:

- Rental Income: Evaluate the current and potential rental income that the property can generate. Consider market rents in the area, vacancy rates, and any potential for rental increases.
- Operating Expenses: Calculate the various operating expenses associated with the property, including property taxes, insurance, maintenance costs, utilities, and property management fees. Make sure to account for any potential increases in these expenses.
- Financing Costs: If you plan to finance the property, consider the interest rate, loan term, and any other associated financing costs. These expenses will impact your cash flow.
- Vacancy Rate: Assess the historical vacancy rate in the area

to estimate potential vacancies and factor this into your cash flow projections.

- Reserves: Set aside a portion of your rental income for future capital expenditures and unexpected expenses. This will help you maintain a positive cash flow even during unforeseen circumstances.

Once you have a clear understanding of the cash flow potential, you can calculate the return on investment (ROI) to determine the profitability of the investment. ROI is a measure of the return as a percentage of the initial investment.

To calculate ROI, use the following formula:

ROI = (Net Profit / Initial Investment) x 100

Net profit is the total income generated from the property after deducting all expenses, including mortgage payments, operating expenses, and vacancies. The initial investment includes the purchase price, closing costs, and any renovation or improvement expenses.

A higher ROI indicates a more profitable investment. However, it's important to consider other factors such as the property's location, potential for appreciation, and future market conditions when making investment decisions.

By carefully analyzing the cash flow potential and ROI of each real estate investment, you can maximize your cash flow and make informed investment decisions that align with your financial goals.

When it comes to financing options for commercial real estate investments, there are several avenues you can explore. Each option has its own advantages and considerations, so it's important to carefully evaluate which one aligns best with your investment goals and financial situation.

1. Traditional Bank Loans:

One of the most common financing options for commercial real estate investments is obtaining a loan from a traditional bank. These loans typically have longer terms and lower interest rates compared to other options. However, they often require a significant down payment and may have stricter eligibility criteria.

2. SBA Loans:

The Small Business Administration (SBA) offers loans specifically designed for small businesses, including those looking to invest in commercial real estate. SBA loans provide favorable terms and lower down payment requirements compared to traditional bank loans. However, the application process can be more complex, and the approval timeline may be longer.

3. Commercial Mortgage-Backed Securities (CMBS):

CMBS loans are a form of financing where multiple commercial mortgages are pooled together and sold as a bond to investors. This option provides flexibility in loan terms and interest rates. However, CMBS loans often require a high credit score and a larger initial investment.

4. Private Lenders:

Private lenders, also known as hard money lenders, offer short-term loans with higher interest rates and more flexible eligibility criteria. This option can be beneficial for investors who need quick financing or have less-than-ideal credit scores. However, the higher interest rates may impact your overall cash flow.

5. Seller Financing:

Seller financing involves the property owner acting as the lender and offering financing options to the buyer. This option can provide more flexibility in terms and eligibility requirements. However, it may be challenging to find sellers willing to offer financing, and the terms may not be as favorable as other options.

6. Crowdfunding:

Crowdfunding platforms allow multiple investors to pool their resources to fund a commercial real estate investment. This option provides an opportunity to invest with a smaller initial capital requirement. However, it's important to carefully evaluate the platform and the investment opportunity to ensure it aligns with your investment goals.

It's recommended to consult with a financial advisor or a mortgage broker to thoroughly understand the advantages and considerations of each financing option before making a decision. Remember, maximizing cash flow from real estate investments requires careful planning and consideration of your financial capabilities.

In order to maximize cash flow from your real estate investments and increase your passive income, it is important to implement strategies that will generate higher returns. Here are some proven strategies that can help you achieve this goal:

**1. Rent Optimization:** One of the most effective ways to increase cash flow is by optimizing rental rates. Research the current market conditions and compare your rental rates to similar properties in the area. If your rates are below market value, consider raising them to generate more income. However, it is important to strike a balance so as not to price yourself out of the market.

**2. Value-Add Improvements:** Making strategic improvements to your properties can increase their value and, in turn, the rental income you can charge. This might include renovating outdated units, adding desirable amenities, or enhancing curb appeal. By investing in these improvements, you can attract higher-quality tenants and justify higher rental rates.

**3. Reduce Vacancy Rates:** Vacant units mean lost income. Implement strategies to minimize vacancy rates, such as effective marketing and tenant retention programs. Ensure your properties are well-maintained, respond promptly to tenant concerns, and offer incentives for lease renewals. By keeping your units occupied, you can maintain a steady cash flow.

**4. Leverage Short-Term Rentals:** Consider utilizing platforms such as Airbnb or VRBO to tap into the short-term rental market. This can be particularly advantageous in high-demand tourist areas or during peak seasons. Short-term rentals often generate higher rental income, but be sure to familiarize yourself with local regulations and potential risks.

**5. Explore Additional Revenue Streams:** Think outside the box and explore additional ways to generate income from your properties. This could include offering storage space for rent, installing vending machines, or providing laundry facilities. These additional revenue streams can significantly boost your cash flow.

**6. Reduce Expenses:** Analyze your expenses and look for areas where you can cut costs without compromising the quality of your properties. For example, negotiate better deals with suppliers, implement energy-saving measures, or consider self-management to save on property management fees.

By implementing these strategies and continuously monitoring your investments, you can maximize cash flow and increase your passive income from real estate. Remember, real estate investing requires careful planning and ongoing evaluation to ensure long-term success.

## Wrapping Up: Achieving Your Goal of Maximizing Cash Flow from Real Estate Investments

As we come to the end of this lesson on commercial real estate investing for beginners, we hope you have gained valuable insights into the world of real estate investment. Our primary focus has been on helping you understand how to maximize cash flow from your investments to increase passive income.

### Importance of Achieving Your Goal

By maximizing cash flow, you can generate a steady stream of income from your real estate investments. This income can provide financial stability, help you achieve your financial goals, and even pave the way for early retirement. It is a crucial element in building long-term wealth and financial freedom.

Remember, achieving your goal of maximizing cash flow requires careful planning, thorough research, and informed decision-making. This lesson has equipped you with the knowledge and tools to make smarter investment choices that align with your financial objectives.

### Continuing Your Learning Journey

If you feel the need to revisit any of the concepts covered in this lesson, we encourage you to review the material again. Take the time to absorb the information fully, as a solid understanding of the fundamentals is key to successful real estate investing.

Additionally, this lesson is just one part of a comprehensive course on commercial real estate investing. We invite you to explore the other lessons in the course to further enhance your knowledge and skills. Each lesson addresses different aspects of real estate investment, providing you with a well-rounded education in this field.

Remember, building wealth through real estate is a journey that requires continuous learning and adaptability. Stay curious, stay informed, and keep honing your expertise. With dedication and persistence, you can achieve your financial goals through real estate investing.

Wishing you success on your real estate investment journey!

# 11

# Network with Experienced Real Estate Investors

One of the key aspects of successful real estate investing is building a strong network of experienced investors. Networking allows you to tap into the knowledge and expertise of those who have already navigated the complexities of the commercial real estate market. By connecting with experienced individuals, you can gain valuable insights, learn from their successes and mistakes, and ultimately accelerate your own progress in the field.

In this lesson, we will guide you through the process of networking with experienced real estate investors. You will learn how to identify potential mentors, attend networking events, join online communities, and leverage social media platforms to connect with professionals in the industry.

By the end of this lesson, you will have the tools and knowledge necessary to start building your own network of experienced real estate investors. So, let's get started on your journey to becoming a successful commercial real estate investor!

Understanding the Importance of Networking in Real Estate

Investing

When it comes to finding profitable real estate deals, networking plays a crucial role in your success. Building a strong network of contacts can provide you with valuable opportunities, insights, and resources that can help you identify and secure profitable investment properties. Here are some key reasons why networking is essential in real estate investing:

**1. Access to Off-Market Deals:** Many of the best real estate investment opportunities are not listed on public platforms or MLS (Multiple Listing Service). Instead, they are often found through word-of-mouth referrals or personal connections. By actively networking with other real estate professionals, you increase your chances of getting access to these off-market deals.

**2. Knowledge Sharing:** Networking allows you to tap into the collective wisdom and experiences of other investors, agents, and industry experts. By engaging in conversations, attending real estate events, and joining online forums or groups, you can learn from others' successes and failures, gain insights into different markets, and stay updated on the latest trends and strategies in real estate investing.

**3. Partnerships and Joint Ventures:** Networking opens doors to potential partnerships and joint ventures. Collaborating with other investors or industry professionals can help you pool resources, share risks, and increase your investment capacity. By teaming up with experienced individuals who complement your skills and expertise, you can tackle larger projects, access better financing options, and maximize your chances of success.

**4. Reliable Referrals:** Through networking, you can establish relationships with trusted professionals such as real estate agents, attorneys, contractors, and property managers. These connections can provide reliable referrals to other professionals or services you may need during your real estate investing journey. Having access to a network of reliable contacts can save you time, money, and potential headaches when it comes to property transactions and management.

**5. Building Your Reputation:** Networking allows you to showcase your knowledge, expertise, and integrity within the real estate community. By actively participating in discussions, sharing valuable insights, and offering assistance to others, you can build a positive reputation as a reliable and knowledgeable investor. This can lead to increased visibility, credibility, and potential joint venture opportunities in the future.

Remember, networking is not just about connecting with others solely for personal gain. It is a two-way street where you should also be willing to offer support, share resources, and provide value to your network. Building genuine relationships and fostering a mutually beneficial network can significantly enhance your chances of finding profitable real estate deals.

Identifying key networking opportunities and events is crucial for finding profitable real estate deals. Networking allows you to connect with industry professionals, potential partners, and experienced investors who can provide valuable insights and opportunities. In this section, we will explore some effective strategies to help you identify and make the most of these networking opportunities.

1. Local Real Estate Associations and Meetups:

Joining local real estate associations and attending meetups is a great way to connect with like-minded individuals and professionals in the industry. These associations often host regular events and meetings where you can meet experienced investors, real estate agents, property managers, and other key players in the field. Make sure to actively participate in discussions, ask questions, and exchange contact information.

2. Real Estate Investment Clubs:

Real estate investment clubs are organizations specifically focused on bringing together investors, both beginners and experienced, to share knowledge and opportunities. These clubs often organize meetings, workshops, and networking events. Look for local real estate investment clubs in your area and consider becoming a member to gain access to valuable resources, education, and networking opportunities.

3. Industry Conferences and Expos:

Attending industry conferences and expos can provide a wealth of networking opportunities. These events bring together professionals, experts, and thought leaders in the real estate industry. Keep an eye out for upcoming conferences and expos in your area or consider traveling to larger events in different cities. Take advantage of the opportunity to engage in conversations, attend relevant sessions, and connect with potential partners or mentors.

4. Online Networking Platforms:

In addition to physical networking events, online platforms can also be a valuable resource for connecting with real estate professionals. Platforms such as LinkedIn, BiggerPockets, and real estate-focused forums provide a space for discussions, sharing experiences, and connecting with potential partners. Join relevant groups, participate in discussions, and reach out to individuals who align with your investment goals.

5. Local Chamber of Commerce:

Consider joining your local Chamber of Commerce to expand your network and connect with business professionals in your area. While not exclusively focused on real estate, the Chamber of Commerce often hosts networking events, business mixers, and seminars that can provide opportunities to meet potential investors and professionals from various industries.

Remember, networking is not just about exchanging business cards or making connections; it's about building relationships and mutually beneficial partnerships. Be proactive, approachable, and genuine in your interactions, and always follow up with contacts afterward to solidify the connection. By actively participating in networking opportunities and events, you increase your chances of finding profitable real estate deals and gaining valuable insights from experienced investors.

In order to find profitable real estate deals, networking events can be an invaluable resource. Attending these events allows you to connect with other professionals in the industry, such as real estate agents, investors, and lenders. Building relationships with these individuals can lead to potential partnerships, access to off-market deals, and valuable industry insights.

Before attending a networking event, it is essential to prepare yourself to make a lasting impression. One of the first steps is to build a personal brand that showcases your expertise and professionalism. Here are some tips to help you prepare:

**1. Define Your Niche:** Determine the specific area of real estate investing that you want to focus on. Whether it's residential properties, commercial buildings, or fix-and-flip projects, having a clear niche will help you establish yourself as an authority in that particular field.

**2. Develop an Elevator Pitch:** Craft a concise and compelling introduction that highlights your unique selling proposition and what sets you apart from other investors. This elevator pitch should be a brief summary of your background, experience, and goals in real estate investing.

**3. Create Professional Business Cards:** Design and print business cards that reflect your personal brand. Include your name, contact information, and any relevant social media profiles or website. Handing out business cards at networking events helps you establish credibility and makes it easier for others to remember you.

**4. Dress Professionally:** Dressing appropriately for networking events shows that you take your real estate investing endeavors seriously. Wear professional attire that aligns with the expectations of the event and ensures you make a positive first impression.

**5. Research Attendees and Presenters:** Prior to the event, research the individuals who will be attending or presenting. This will help you identify potential connections and conversation starters. Showing genuine interest in others' work can lead to meaningful conversations and opportunities.

**6. Practice Active Listening:** During networking events, focus on actively listening to others rather than solely promoting yourself. Engage in meaningful conversations, ask questions, and show genuine interest in what others have to say. Building relationships is a two-way street, and actively listening can help you establish trust and rapport.

**7. Follow Up:** After the event, follow up with the individuals you connected with to solidify the relationship. Send personalized emails or connect on professional networking platforms such as LinkedIn. Building and maintaining relationships is an ongoing process, and following up demonstrates your commitment to cultivating mutually beneficial connections.

By effectively preparing for networking events and building a strong personal brand, you increase your chances of finding profitable real estate deals. Remember to be authentic, professional, and proactive in your networking efforts, as these qualities will help you stand out in a competitive industry.

Approaching experienced real estate investors and initiating conversations is a valuable strategy for finding profitable real estate deals. By engaging with those who have already established themselves in the industry, you can gain insights, knowledge, and potentially even partner on investment opportunities.

Here are a few steps to help you approach experienced real estate investors:

1. Research and Identify Potential Investors: Start by researching and identifying successful real estate investors in your target market. Look for individuals who have a proven track record of successful investments and align with your investment goals.
2. Attend Real Estate Networking Events: Networking events provide a great opportunity to meet and connect with experienced investors. Attend local real estate meetups, conferences, and seminars to expand your network and initiate conversations.
3. Introduce Yourself: When approaching an experienced investor, introduce yourself confidently. Be prepared with a brief elevator pitch that highlights your interest in real estate investing and your goals. Show genuine interest in their work and accomplishments.
4. Ask Thoughtful Questions: Engage in meaningful conversations by asking thoughtful questions about their investment strategies, preferred markets, and property types. This will not only demonstrate your interest but also give you valuable insights into their approach.
5. Offer Value: Show that you are willing to contribute and add

value to their investment endeavors. Share any relevant skills, resources, or connections that you may have. This will help establish a mutually beneficial relationship.

6. Build Relationships: Building relationships takes time, so be patient and persistent. Follow up with individuals you meet and maintain regular communication. Offer to assist them with any projects or research that aligns with your expertise.

7. Seek Mentorship or Partnership: If you have built a strong rapport with an experienced investor, don't hesitate to ask for mentorship or partnership opportunities. Many successful investors are willing to share their knowledge and may even be open to partnering on deals.

Approaching experienced real estate investors and initiating conversations can be intimidating at first, but it is an essential step towards finding profitable real estate deals. Remember to be respectful, genuine, and eager to learn from their experiences. With time and effort, you can establish valuable relationships that can significantly contribute to your real estate investing journey.

When it comes to finding profitable real estate deals, one of the most valuable tools at your disposal is networking. Building relationships with other professionals in the industry can open doors to opportunities and help you tap into their knowledge and expertise. In this section, we will explore how to maximize the value of networking through effective follow-up and relationship building.

1. **Follow Up:** After attending networking events or meeting potential partners, it is crucial to follow up promptly. Send a personalized email or make a phone call expressing your

interest in continuing the conversation. This demonstrates your professionalism and commitment. Additionally, it helps to schedule a meeting or coffee to discuss potential collaborations or exchange ideas.

2. **Stay in Touch:** Building relationships is an ongoing process, so it's essential to stay in touch with your network regularly. Send occasional emails or make phone calls to check in, share industry news, or invite them to events or webinars you think may interest them. This consistent communication helps to strengthen the bond and ensure that you remain top-of-mind when opportunities arise.

3. **Attend Industry Events:** Make it a priority to attend industry conferences, seminars, and networking events. These gatherings offer a great platform to meet like-minded individuals, potential partners, and key players in the commercial real estate market. Take advantage of these opportunities to expand your network, learn from others, and showcase your expertise.

4. **Join Real Estate Groups:** Joining real estate groups, both online and offline, can provide valuable connections and knowledge. Participate actively in discussions, share insights, and ask questions. By engaging with the group, you can establish yourself as a knowledgeable and trustworthy professional, which can lead to potential partnerships or deals.

5. **Offer Value:** Networking is a two-way street. It's not just about what others can do for you; it's also about what you can offer in return. Share your expertise, offer assistance, and provide value to others in your network. By being a helpful and resourceful member of the community, you can build stronger relationships and gain the trust of potential partners or investors.

By maximizing the value of networking through effective

follow-up and relationship building, you can significantly increase your chances of finding profitable real estate deals. Remember, real estate investing is a people business, and the strength of your network can greatly impact your success.

## Summary

In conclusion, if you are interested in investing in real estate, it is crucial to remember the importance of networking with experienced real estate investors to gain valuable industry insights. This lesson has provided you with an understanding of the benefits of networking and the various ways you can connect with experienced investors. By building relationships and learning from those who have already achieved success in the industry, you can greatly enhance your own investment journey.

## Next Steps

If you need to review any part of this lesson, feel free to go back and revisit the content. Additionally, don't forget to explore the other lessons available in this course. Each lesson covers different aspects of commercial real estate investing and will provide you with further knowledge and guidance to help you achieve your investment goals.

Remember, investing in real estate can be a rewarding and lucrative endeavor, but it requires continuous learning, networking, and staying updated with industry trends. By utilizing the valuable resources available to you, such as this course, you are taking important steps towards becoming a successful real estate investor. Good luck on your investment journey!

# Congratulations on Completing the Commercial Real Estate Investing for Beginners Course!

## You've Taken a Bold Step Towards Financial Success

As you reach the end of this self-guided online course, we want to commend you on your commitment and dedication to expanding your knowledge and venturing into the world of commercial real estate investing. By completing this course, you have taken a significant step towards achieving your financial goals and securing a prosperous future.

Throughout the course, you have gained essential insights into the fundamentals of commercial real estate investing. You have learned about the various types of commercial properties, analyzed market trends, examined financing options, and explored strategies for maximizing returns on your investments.

We hope that the knowledge you have acquired will empower you to make informed decisions and navigate the complexities of the commercial real estate market with confidence. Remember, investing in commercial real estate can be a lucrative endeavor, but it requires careful planning, thorough research, and a willingness to adapt to changing market conditions.

Now that you have completed the course, it's time to put your newfound knowledge into action. Start exploring potential investment opportunities, network with industry professionals, and seek guidance from experienced mentors. Remember, continuous learning and staying updated with market trends will be paramount to your success as a commercial real estate investor.

Lastly, we want to express our gratitude for choosing this course as your learning resource. We genuinely hope that the material covered has exceeded your expectations and provided you with the tools necessary to embark on your commercial real estate investing journey. Remember, success in this field comes to those who are proactive, persistent, and innovative.

Once again, congratulations on completing the Commercial Real Estate Investing for Beginners course! We wish you the best of luck in all your future endeavors and hope to hear about your successes in the exciting world of commercial real estate investing.

Leave us a book review on Amazon for free real estate gear to help you along your journey!

Resources: commercialrealestateinvestingforbeginners.com